GW00544228

THE UNFOLDING JOURNEY

THE UNFOLDING JOURNEY

ELIZABETH FARRELL

PELEGRIN TRUST
in association with
PILGRIM BOOKS
TASBURGH · NORWICH · ENGLAND

British Library Cataloguing in Publication Data
Farrell, Elizabeth, *1921–*
The unfolding journey.
1. Spiritualism. Mediums. Farrell, Elizabeth 1921–
I. Title II. Pelegrin Trust
133.91092

ISBN 0–946259–35–6

Photoset by Waveney Typesetters, Norwich
and printed in Great Britain at the University Press, Cambridge

CONTENTS

For my family

ACKNOWLEDGEMENT

I would like to express my warmest thanks to Mr Paul Beard for his invaluable support and encouragement throughout the past years.

Without the wisdom of his guidance this book would not have been written.

Elizabeth Farrell

INTRODUCTION

FEW PROFESSIONS ARE less understood than that of mediumship. Although much that is required for mediumistic skills is paralleled in other caring professions, its most important factor – the source of its material – cannot be learned except by experience, nor can it be guaranteed even by disciplined work. Many would like to become mediums in the mistaken notion that it leads to an easy glamour and power. These would shrink from the emotional hardships involved.

Like many forms of art, mediumship requires both a natural gift, and also a disciplined training. Its reward mainly lies in the fruits it bears for other people's problems, difficulties and heart-aches. To qualify for giving such help, mediums have nearly always first undergone similar blows in their own personal life, and have learned some of the lessons these impose. Hardship and loss provide valuable training, often before any formal training begins. It is by such a route that mediums are often forced to qualify, as well as by the taxing self-disciplines needed for their specific role. It requires, too, a medium to develop a potential medium, because only a medium is able to perceive the true sources of the information produced by her pupils.

The Unfolding Journey is one of the very best accounts we

have of the working life of a medium. Its unfailing honesty and frankness enable us to stand, as it were, by Mrs Farrell's side as she describes her particular early difficulties, which spared her nothing. These include the experience of becoming obsessed – not by an evil spirit, though these certainly exist – but by a nun, suffering her own purgatories resulting from inadequacies of character in her life on earth. Elizabeth Farrell unveils the inch by inch struggle over months to overcome this obsession and to establish her own true self, and then to maintain her identity at new deeper levels.

Later, she describes with equal honesty the spiritual help and kindness she received from fellow mediums, and then from her own discarnate spiritual teacher, Nemerah, some of whose philosophy will be found in the later pages. His teaching is essentially non-dogmatic, and very much in tune with what many teachers, both on earth and from the inner world, are now expressing in order to prepare mankind for the coming Aquarian age. Nemerah is a hard task-master, but with a deep kindness behind his sternness alike towards Elizabeth herself and to her clients, and tinged also with humour in the disciplining.

This book is not a piece of propaganda on behalf of mediumship. It is essentially an autobiography, written with every intention of telling the whole truth as she sees it. Pitfalls and rewards are dealt with alike. It opens up for the reader a fuller understanding of how mediumship really works – altogether more subtly than most suppose – and of the problems, skills, and strength of character needed. In days to come, mediumship is likely to be regarded with greater respect and admiration than it receives today, though well deserved by the serious practitioners of this taxing caring profession.

Paul Beard

PART ONE

EARLY EXPERIENCES

SOME ARE BORN MEDIUMS, some achieve mediumship, some have mediumship thrust upon them and I place myself in the second category. For the last thirteen or fourteen years my work has been mainly centred at the College of Psychic Studies. I was asked to go there in 1974, by the then President Mr Paul Beard and it is at his suggestion and that of Miss Rosamund Lehmann, also at the request of many of my students, that I write the story of my own beginnings.

I have often spoken of them, both from the platform and also in various instructions that I give when I am teaching. My acceptance of mediumship and the experience of my initiation into that acceptance were both difficult and at times traumatic. It is hard to retrace in retrospect the various threads of a tapestry that eventually weave together to form a picture.

I wish to write with complete honesty and frankness. In so doing it is inevitable that my weaknesses and personal inadequacies at the time will damn me in the eyes of some readers. For the psychologist and the analyst the 'labels' are plainly there.

My immediate entry into the realms of the mind was both painful and difficult, leaving me often bewildered and hopeless. I now look back on that time as invaluable in terms of the process of growth.

It must be understood that everyone accepting mediumship does not have to undergo my particular ordeals. Each initiation is different according to the complexity of the personality, our egocentricity, our emotional balance, our type of mind; all will play their part. Above all, the quality of our self-discipline and spiritual aspiration will determine the type of mediumship we attain.

Almost always there is hardship to be borne at some level, perhaps physical disability, lack of means, childhood deprivation, or spiritual isolation. Very often a medium is called upon to give up something very precious. These hard lessons take place because we have consciously to accept that part of our life is under direction from a force of love, wisdom and intelligence higher than our own. We may rebel against it, but ultimately recognise and value the truth it shows us.

Some readers may glance over the early pages of this book and dismiss me with a 'label'. Some of you I hope will continue, and observe that my difficulties were really beautifully placed stepping stones without which any subsequent development would not have taken place.

I will begin with the first truly memorable psychic experience I had, which was in 1960 at the death of my father. At that time I was a very happy woman. My life centred entirely round my home, my children, my animals. The death of my father was the first experience I had of deep personal loss. He had been a tea planter in Ceylon. My childhood up to the age of ten-and-a-half was one that I look upon with great gratitude and with a sense of increased awareness of the magical affect it had, and still continues to have, upon my life, magical in the sense in which children are able to accept things as magical. Therefore my life up to that time was one of acceptance. I did not consciously relate to the beauty around me then, but absorbed it unknowingly. The memories I have of that time are beautiful and thought-provoking still. As I recall scenes from that part of my life they are intensely vivid in colour and brilliance. The child I was then I am now able to relive in the growth of my adulthood and understanding. That is why I think of that part of my life as magical. It lives within me and continues to grow and carry its impact through the years.

My father was a truly Christian man and for him his life was governed and guided by those principles. He taught me the Bible. I remember as a very small child waking to find him praying by my bedside. He told me the Bible stories in a simple, meaningful way; he taught me the Lord's Prayer. We lived on a tea estate and therefore our life was to a degree governed by distance and we didn't often go to church but until I went to school the concept of the Christ and an all-seeing God was utterly part of my life.

I recall listening to a sermon, at about six years old, which had something to do with the second coming of Christ. I determined that I would watch the sky at every possible moment, so that I would not miss his descent.

There were only two occasions in my childhood when I was touched by spirit. Both happened between five and six years old. One was very beautiful. I was sleeping in a large drop-sided cot. I felt quite a sharp tap on the top of my head, which woke me instantly. I had no sense of alarm. Sitting on the rails of the cot were three angels – their faces quite clear – one surrounded by a soft yellow light, one pink, and one blue. I told no-one, not even my father. The recollection is still vivid, though I realise now that the effect of wings was probably the auric field surrounding spirit people of advanced spirituality.

On the second occasion I was walking in the garden and I heard my name called three times quite clearly. I knew no-one was near. I was unnerved, and ran back to the house. One day I told this to an Aunt. She was ultra-religious and perhaps not very wise in her dealing with an imaginative child. Staying with her later, once more I was suddenly wakened during the night, this time to see a black figure kneeling by my bed. It took me a few seconds to realise it was only my Aunt in a black evening dress. She said 'Betty, if you ever hear that voice again, you must say "Speak Lord for thy child heareth".' When she had gone I buried my head under the bed-clothes, my heart beating, absolutely determined that I wouldn't listen to any voices that didn't belong to people I could see!

As I grew older my attitude towards religious observance changed. As was usual in those days, between ten and eleven years old I was sent to school in England. This meant a separation from parents for a period of about five years, a very traumatic transition for the children. It was long afterwards before I understood the price parents paid.

I went to a small boarding school in Plymouth, spending holidays with relations. Desperately unhappy at first, I adjusted and enjoyed my time there. One summer, through arrangements made by the school, my brother and I were sent with others to spend the summer with people who managed the Duke of Bedford's estate near Tavistock. It was a wonderful holiday for children. Did the sun really shine every day? It was here I saw my first ghost. I slept in a small room overlooking the staircase, by myself. I lay in bed sleepily listening to the hum of adult voices below. The room was quite dark. I was aware of growing terror, someone was in the room with me. I forced myself out of bed rushing blindly for the door and with relief saw the light from the downstair hall where it reached the landing. I knelt to fix the door open with a doorstop, and then I froze. Blacker than the shadows behind me was the cowled figure of a monk standing by my side. The emanation was not nice. It seemed an age before he went. I reached the bed, and lay sleepless, ice-cold and trembling for the rest of the night, a hymn-book on my chest (the only remotely religious object I had). I did not tell anyone, fearful of ridicule, but always slept with the door open from then on.

When I was fourteen came another change. I lived with relations permanently, going daily to grammar school. Gradually I began to question beliefs I had accepted. Because I could not equate that which I had been taught with what I could physically see and understand I threw, as it were, 'the baby out with the bath water', denying the whole existence of a life after death.

For a while, I called myself a Humanist. I did believe that we should do what we could with this life for good but I also believed very firmly and strongly that it was the only one I had.

Therefore when my father died, in 1960, and I was at the crematorium for the service, I had nobody to whom I could pray. I was aware, as I knelt there, that I was losing perhaps my best friend. I thought of the many many years of love, kindness, generosity, teaching and giving that I had received at the hands of this man. My life would not be changed greatly at his death. For those whom I then held most dear were still with me. There were so many memories running through my mind, so many feelings of regret that I hadn't done and said and shown more, as we all feel when those we love pass. I had no way to ease my emotional pain. Thus in my need, I opened my heart and said within myself, from the heart, 'If there is anything please take care of this very good man.'

I was then aware of being filled with utter peace and enlargement. I knew without a shadow of doubt that I had been heard and was being listened to. Many people will have had such experiences. It is one of utter joy that comes with a spiritual door being opened. My sorrow left me. I felt at peace and wholly comforted. It was about six weeks later that I had my first truly memorable psychic occurrence.

I awoke one morning to find myself standing by my bedside looking down at myself and my husband asleep. I realised that I had been woken by the sound of the back door bell. I ran along the passage, down the stairs and into our kitchen. Standing in the kitchen was my father. It was a truly joyful reunion. He enfolded me in his arms, as he always did. I could feel the slight roughness of his cheek as I touched it and smell the mist on his raincoat. It was a raincoat that he had refused to throw away, very old and worn and dear to him which two or three weeks before he died, I had mended, washed and cleaned. I cannot remember the exact things that he said but it amounted to the fact that I was right and to go on looking, he was all right and I was correct in my understanding that he still existed, to go on looking and find out for myself, something to that effect. I can't remember quite how he went but I know he went out of the back door. I don't remember either how I got back upstairs but I do remember very clearly looking down again at the two bodies and saying to myself: 'I've got to get back in there.' On re-awaking in the usual way, because I had smelt the faint mist on his raincoat I looked out of the window and it was indeed a cold misty dawn.

When these things happened to me, I was unable to understand them. It was many years later before they made sense. I now know that we do leave our bodies during the sleep state and at that time we are totally functional in a different dimension. Therefore my father and I were solid to each other at that time. Since then I have only had one or two equally vivid astral experiences but when they happened I had more awareness of what was happening to me.

Now at this stage many things came together. First of all my husband was in business and it fell to our part very often to be entertained and to entertain other executives. It was on one such an occasion that I came to meet Nicky Murray, who until very recently was the custodian of the Bach Flower

Remedy Centre. We were being entertained by Malcolm Murray, Nicky's husband. I remember the occasion very well. We met for dinner in a club in London and we were to go on to a play. When we met, Malcolm said his wife would be late. He explained that she was a spiritual healer and was working that evening at the Spiritualist Association of Great Britain. He said she would be with us later for dinner. I was highly intrigued at this. Nicky duly arrived as arranged. So began the first of many conversations that led to my deep interest in the subject.

I told Nicky of the experience that I had had and she subsequently introduced my husband and me to Ursula Roberts and her husband Sidney Richardson. We went to their home for a teaching by Ursula's guide Ramadan. When it was over Ursula turned to me and said 'You are a clairvoyant, you should do something about it.' Neither my husband nor I could accept this, we looked at each other in some amusement and then forgot about it.

The next few years continued very much as before but I did begin to read avidly. I remember being very impressed by *The Rock of Truth* by Arthur Findlay. Most particularly I was moved by the autobiography of Estelle Roberts, *Forty Years a Medium*. After reading it, remembering what had happened at the funeral of my father, I rather dramatically took the book between my two hands. From the core of my being I opened up in the same way and said from my heart: 'If this is true let me find out.' And I did.

I continued to see Nicky Murray, to learn a great deal from her and she became a very close personal friend. In September of 1964 I found myself with a lot of extra time. In the natural course of events both my children had gone to boarding school. My husband still worked eighteen hours a day, but my job had been halved.

I took a part-time clerical job in the mornings, from 9 o'clock until 1 p.m. and I decided then to investigate for myself. I went to various Spiritualist churches and up to the Spiritualist Association of Great Britain. I made up my mind, that if it was possible I would join a development circle, which I did. I realise now that I lacked humility in my approach, that I was judgmental and intolerant as ill-informed people often are when approaching a subject of which they know nothing. I saw many trance mediums at that time and would have none of any of them until I heard Ivy Northage in trance. Listening to her guide Chan, I knew that I had found something rare and beautiful. I knew that I had found my teacher for that time and was truly delighted when I was accepted as part of the development class.

PART TWO

A PLUNGE INTO DANGEROUS TERRITORY

I SHOULD EXPLAIN here that at that time I was physically ill and also that I was full of fear. At this stage I will not explain where this fear came from but I was always afraid. The fears were deeply hidden of course. But I had also read that people developing psychically sometimes have unpleasant experiences and somehow deep down within me I knew that I should be one of them. I shook this off and felt that under such strong guidance nothing like this could happen to me. I went to class for three weeks. I found the whole thing very fascinating. In class under tuition, we learned to open the psychic centres or chakras to extra psychic energy, also learning which psychic centre governed a particular psychic ability. We call this 'opening up'. Nothing much happened to me. I would go home and discuss it with my husband and my mother and say 'You know, they're lovely people but they talk about seeing this and feeling that, I feel absolutely nothing!'

Now I was, as I have mentioned, ill at the time. I was over twelve stone and suffered very much from rheumatism and was nearly always in pain of some kind. I didn't make much fuss of any of this but very often I could only get downstairs sideways holding on to the bannister, moving one foot at a time until my general circulation and pain became manageable. I had had two bad operations. The doctor had said I mustn't lift for six months and so on, and not do this and not do that, none of which was practical. Sometimes all of this would catch up on me and I would feel very ill and very weak. On the fourth week I felt very much like this. However, I went to class and Ivy Northage looked at me and commented on how ill I looked and she wouldn't allow me to work, or try to work. After the class was over another member came over to me and suggested she gave me healing. I realise now that what happened was that I unwittingly opened my psychic centres again. I was very inexperienced and I didn't understand that the state I was in and the fact that I was unaware of my latent psychism, made me very vulnerable to any earthbound entities that were around, and could attach themselves to my auric field.

We were alone in the room and that is what must have happened. During class I was alright because we 'opened' and 'closed' our psychic centres in a disciplined way. Perhaps the healer, also inexperienced, didn't know that a patient's psychic centre must also be 'sealed' at the end of a healing session. After she had gone – she was a kind person – I remained in the room alone, and was assailed by an overwhelming feeling of melancholia, a sense of utter desolation which remained with me as I left the building to take the train home.

I must have stayed for some other activity, because the class was held in the afternoon and it was quite late when I reached my destination. I slipped from the station into beautiful clear moonlight. Touched by the clarity of the sky, wonderfully my heaviness of heart lifted and I began the walk home.

Without warning I had a revelation of complete and utter love. I was immersed in it. For that moment I felt I understood what love really was. I knew that it was far greater than my feeling for any single human being, that love is a force that far outstrips our concept of time, and that we all belong to a much greater reality. For a moment I felt I could understand eternity with my soul. It is not possible to put this into words. I have never experienced quite such a moment since. I felt altered and I knew that I would never be the same again. I understood that prayer was giving, I understood that for me God was something I couldn't explain or understand but I knew existed. I was aware of a universal power of love, light and creativity, a strength of being within myself, knowing that I belonged to part of a whole which I couldn't explain and couldn't understand, but in which I had complete trust. I realised that my love, as I had understood it before, was a puny, infinitesimal thing beside it but because I had love of a kind, as all human beings have, there is part of me that is of God and as such I knew then that in some inescapable way I must go through with whatever lay ahead.

During the next week I began to hear voices and these voices told me that if I had faith and followed instruction I would be a wonderful medium. I was told that when I went up to class again, as I came out of the station I would see a member of the class in front of me. I was to follow her, as soon as I got inside the door at the S.A.G.B. to give her my coat which was heavy, go into the Chapel, wait there until it was time for class. During class I was told I would go into trance, somthing would go wrong, I would fall and would be caught by the only male member of the class.

On the way up, in the train, I began to feel like a nun. I wiped the traces of lipstick off my face and took my earrings off and once more I had the same feeling of terrible depression. As I came out of the station there was one of the members of the class just in front of me. If I had known a little more I'd have pulled myself up, beause it was not the right woman. It was, however, a member of the class. So I followed my instructions; I was feeling very ill, I just about made my way to the foyer, I had no energy and was very short of breath. There was no way I could have climbed the stairs wearing that heavy coat. I asked this woman to take my coat into class for me. I went up to the Chapel and knelt in front of a big brass cross that was there. This was totally against anything I would normally have done. I heard somebody come in, it must have looked odd because they went out again rather hurriedly. For me the whole thing was quite out of character. I sat down and quite suddenly I could neither open my eyes nor speak. At a few minutes before the time for class I got up and without opening my eyes walked into the room where we had the circle and sat down. I heard everyone come in and their hushed voices. They must have been very frightened. I still thought something wonderful would happen and that I would produce a trance control of great beauty. I had no feeling of fear at this time. I heard everything that was said. I could hear that they were frightened. Then I heard Mrs Northage come in and say: 'Oh no', and I heard her run for help up the stairs to the healing section. I then became very cold and very very frightened. I felt as though I had a weight like a rock on my back and my shoulders began to sag. It was physical in effect, I couldn't keep my shoulders up. Mrs Northage came back into the room and I heard a man's voice say: 'Can we get her upstairs.' We used to take off our shoes for circle and mine were off. I felt Mrs Northage kneeling at my feet and heard her saying: 'Help me put your shoes on, dear.' I got them on and stood up and as I did so, I fell. I was caught by the healer, not the member of the circle. This was the second incident incorrectly foretold. I have learnt since that if you are not working properly everything is slightly off key, that when you are influenced as I was from a lower strata of spirit energy then things are never quite right and sometimes very wrong indeed. However, I didn't know that then.

The healers on duty that day were Albert Denton and his

son Peter. A little while previously I had seen Albert Denton. He had a hearty cheerful manner, hail-fellow-well-met, and I at that time couldn't bear this expansive approach. I had said to myself in effect, 'That's one healer I'll never come to.' How they got me up the stairs I don't know. I was on my feet but they had to support me, half dragging me and I was so so cold with this awful weight bowing me down. They got me on to the healing couch and I heard Peter say to his father, 'What on earth is it?' And Albert said, 'God knows, sudden emotional stress I suppose.' 'What shall we do?' 'I don't know, you take her legs and I'll do the head and arms.' I have never since felt anything quite like it. It was as though waves of warm current flowed into me and my body began to feel warm and then I could open my eyes and eventually sit up.

Albert Denton said, 'Can you tell us what has happened?' I replied 'No.' Then with a great effort I said: 'I feel I want to ask you to forgive me.' Kind man that he was, he answered, 'I have nothing to forgive but of course friend I forgive you freely.' I felt the weight fall off my back, literally the pressure went. I could lift my head and straighten my shoulders. It reminds me of the bundle falling off the back of Christian in *The Pilgrim's Progress*!

I then went down to class, and banged on the door, once more out of character, this absolute determination that I should be in class, that's where I belonged, my greatest friends were there and they would understand all that had happened to me. Instead someone came to the door and I was handed my things and told that it would be better if I didn't sit, but that Ivy would come and see me later after class. This she did. Kindly but firmly she told me I could not continue with the class. I was emotionally deeply shocked and found the outcome unbelievable. I realise in retrospect now, that she was absolutely right. I was, in that state, a danger to other members of the class, and since then I have had to take such decisions myself.

I managed to get home fairly reasonably. One of the members of the class was very kind and offered to drive me but by then I wanted to be left alone. When I got home, in the middle of supper, I broke down and started to weep, I felt utterly alone. Ashamed of the awful spectacle I had made of myself, I would not tell either my husband or my mother what had really happened but only that I was never going back. I was at that time also going through the change of life and I think they both thought that this was part of it. It also made my husband feel very opposed to my having anything further to do with the subject.

The next day I sent for Nicky Murray and asked her 'Nicky am I mad?' 'Bless you no,' she said. 'You're very psychic, tell me exactly what happened.' Then she said, 'You know, that nun is still here, you've been obsessed by a nun still close to the earth, that's what's happened.' I remembered how I continually wanted to ask forgiveness, how I'd literally thrown myself in front of the cross, as I had seen other nuns do. Bits of the puzzle began to fall into place. Then Nicky said, 'You have to get rid of her; ask for help and you'll be shown the way.' She and another close friend came every afternoon to see me, to talk to me, one or the other every day for a week, after that once a week for weeks on end. Nicky accepted it all but my other friend told me subsequently she was terrified. She knew nothing of the subject except what she understood from Nicky and she was sure that I would have to go into a Mental Home. I thought I was going to die but that came later. I prayed for help to get rid of the nun but I didn't pray in the accepted sense; I just talked to the people I knew were listening, and I was no longer aware of her presence.

Between September 1964 and January 1965 I had the most extensive and varied psychic experiences to date. I have long since lost their continuity. Several types of phenomena were concurrent. I was subjected to them constantly, the most spectacular usually during the night or early hours of the morning, about 3 a.m. I usually slept about three hours very deeply, out of sheer exhaustion, from about midnight, and that was nearly always all the sleep I had during the night over this period. Some of the things that happened I will remember with joy all my life, some, so beautiful, I shall not attempt to put on paper, they are too personal. Others perhaps can best be forgotten.

When Nicky told me that I must get rid of the nun this frightened me because I felt that I had already done so. One night some weeks after I had left the S.A.G.B. my husband and I were in the sitting room. He was asleep, the electric fire was on, also two lamps. Sitting there very lonely and unhappy trying to make sense of it all I was attracted by the fact that, due to the light combination, the cretonne covers were reflecting as patterns on the back of a highly polished leather chair in one corner. As I looked the pattern started to move and blend making pictures, forming face after face, quite different, a soldier with his eyes bandaged, a woman with an old-fashioned hairstyle and white collar, eyes tightly closed; these are two I remember vividly. All these faces had one thing in common, all were blind. 'Who do I know who is blind?' I went back in my thoughts to my childhood to one old lady who had taken a fancy to me when I was about seven years old. I was fascinated at the time because she was looked after by a Chinese girl whose name was Chan! The moment I registered the name everything stopped and became normal. Chan was the only spirit teacher at that time I knew. I really understood that in some way Chan would help me. This is a wonderful story of goodness from the spirit people. I've often told it and each time I do I am moved.

The next night my husband was not at home so when everyone else was in bed I came down and put the fire and lamps on, exactly as the night before, and sat quietly waiting. I knew that whatever happened would happen in that chair.

Gradually I could see first a cross build up, bright light first of all and then a cross. It formed in the back of the chair and then moved forward and then slowly the black and white robes of a nun formed behind it so that the cross was on her breast. I could see her quite clearly sitting in the chair but not her face. I seemed to know what to say. 'You want to be forgiven? I cannot do that, I haven't the right but if you will say the Lord's Prayer with me someone will come who can.' I was told to go and kneel by her chair. I did so but as I moved towards her I could no longer see her, the molecular structure had been changed by the distance. I could still feel her quite solidly as I knelt and began to say the Prayer, I had got half way through when there was a flash of light and everything electric in the house fused.

My mother whose room was above, banged with a stick on the ceiling. She had apparently been reading late, which she often did. 'What's happened?' she called. 'My lights and fire have gone out.' I mended the fuses very shakily. The nun had gone.

I reiterate, it is difficult to write a consistent account because there were so many facets running concurrently on several levels, both during the day and night. At the physical level I found it, as I have said, very difficult to walk. I used to walk to work and I could only go about fifty yards, if as much as that, without having to stop for breath and during this time I was also subjected, while at work, to the most harrowing physical developments. I would try to bear, without showing it, being banged hard down my spine. I physically felt it. Sometimes it would be so bad that I would have to get up and go into the cloakroom. Attempting to work in those conditions, never knowing what was going to happen to me at any particular time, was very difficult indeed.

A few days after my collapse I was aware that I could see Sidney Richardson, who had been President of the Spiritualist Association, a well known healer and, as I have mentioned previously, Ursula Robert's husband. He had died a year or so previously. I had only met him the once at their home and seen him once, only from a distance. When I had seen him he was then in charge of Ursula's healing clinic which then ran every Friday at the Spiritualist Association. I couldn't understand two things; one that he should come to me and secondly that although he was there to help me he obviously didn't know who I was from Adam. I realised long afterwards that my name must have been put on the absent healing list at the Spiritualist Association and Sidney Richardson was still continuing to work for them in his status of spirit healer. I saw him every day for about six weeks. He would sometimes appear in a white healer's coat and sometimes in a navy blue suit. When he went he would often pat me on the shoulder and say: 'You'll be all right.' Long afterwards I checked with Ursula and she said that this was a very significant habit of his with his patients. He put me on a diet and for three weeks I ate nothing but Granny Smith apples and a consommé soup. He stressed that I must eat the skins because the chewing was important. I lost about 20 lbs. Then gradually he told me what to eat, little by little, until I could eat normally again.

My husband was often away at this time, luckily, for it would have been an impossible situation otherwise. My mother, often badly frightened, was unfailing in her support. She was sure I was going out of my mind. She did everything she could to help with the running of the home and to look after me. Sometimes, between midnight and 3 a.m. in despair, crying at all I was going through, I would suddenly hear, or rather sense, a kind of high pitched vibration. In the corner of the room where I was sitting there would appear a red candle and I would hear Sidney Richardson say: 'I've brought my wife' and I would know that Ursula was in the room. I could see neither of them on these occasions but heard their voices quite distinctly. I didn't know Ursula Roberts in those days, I had just met her the once. She would talk to me, quite as she would when I met her later, discuss anything I cared to talk about. She was asleep, Sidney Richardson dead and I, wide awake and alive! When they went the candle in the corner of the room would fade away.

During this period, Gordon Turner, the well-known healer, appeared in my bedroom. I had only seen him once and then from a distance on the very day I had the traumatic breakdown at the Centre. I had been coming down the stairs to go home, he was standing at the desk at the bottom and he looked up and gave me a smile full of warmth and kindness and it had helped. When he appeared to me now he spoke quite rationally. We spoke, I remember, about electric shock treatment for mental patients which he hated. When I met him, I never actually talked to him about this but after his death many years later this was substantiated by one of his friends whom I met. She told me that this was indeed the case, that he did have a very strong feeling against this particular type of treatment. He said that it affected the aura around the patient. When he came to me I was shocked because he was quite explicit in some of the things he said and I felt, in the state I was in, that all healers should be 'holier than thou' and thought that it must be some darkness inside myself and I was once more distraught. Later when I got to know Gordon he was the sweetest and most compassionate of men. He had a marvellous sense of humour but would on occasions be quite crude, in fact exactly as he was. He must have been asleep when he came to me, or else doing his own absent healing which he used to do for four hours every night. People wrote to him from all over the world. He was also a wonderful animal healer, having a deep love of animals.

It was about this time that one night I was woken as usual about 3 a.m. The room was suffused in a strange soft light.

Sapphy, my beloved poodle, was asleep at the bottom of my bed and and she started to moan. I sat up and began to stroke her. Suddenly the bed sagged with additional weight and instead of little Sapphy there was a large black spaniel lying there. Its front paw was doubled up. I took it gently between my hands and I heard myself say, 'It isn't broken.' I felt it very carefully and deeply embedded between the pads was a long thorn which I drew out very gently. Then there was a type of shudder, the light disappeared. Sapphy lay sleeping peacefully, I was sitting upright in a dark room but I knew, somewhere, a dog would be well by next morning.

There was one night when I felt the animals of their own knowledge and love protected me. I was in a state of abject fear, so afraid I could not turn off the bedroom light, or lie down. Sapphy as usual lay by my left side. The door not quite shut was pushed open. Our very large dog Toby entered followed by the cat. He jumped up and lay across the bottom of the bed, simultaneously the white cat laid herself along the right side. I had the sense of being consciously guarded. I lay down and slept.

I have since learnt that animals do have a slower frequency rate than our own. Of their own choice they remain near the the earth when they die, near to the people they have loved so selflessly and served so faithfully, unaware of any alteration in their circumstances, except in their renewed vitality.

Less frequently these days, it is true, but since her death I have often felt Sapphy jump on to my bed just before I fall asleep.

One morning I felt very ill but for some reason I started to sing and out came the most glorious voice. I sang *The Lost Chord* and I sang an extra verse that I didn't know. It was completely effortless and the verse appropriate. I have never been able to recall it since, but for the second time I was outside my body looking down at myself sitting on the floor.

There was one other occasion when a voice sang through

me. It happened in Church. I began to sing the hymn. Instead of my voice, out came a man's beautiful baritone. It created quite a lot of attention around me!

Then came a morning I shall never forget. It was a Saturday and the family were all at home for the week-end. I came down feeling so ill that I thought to myself 'I am dying.' I saw everyone off to their various activities, my mother went out and I crawled step by step up the stairs and somehow got on to the bed. I had no strength, no breath. Sapphy curled up by me, she knew something was wrong, she knew and she wouldn't leave me but couldn't stay close. She started to cry and went to the end of the bed. I felt myself go out through the top of my head. I seemed attached just by the eyes, and somehow knew I had a choice. No-one would force me either way. Strangely, partly I wanted to go, I felt warm and safe, totally unafraid where I had been so frightened and so alone. It would be so easy. It is difficult to express the sense of illumination and light. I would be so easy just to let go. But I thought how awful it would be for my husband and the children, it wouldn't be fair. A voice said 'Alright, get up and fight.' I got up and walked backwards and forwards the width of the room, seemingly for hours, until gradually I felt strength and movement coming back to me in full measure and I was able to go downstairs and make myself a cup of tea.

When my husband died less than two years later, I was so overwhelmingly grateful that I had made that decision, otherwise the girls would have been without both of us. I understood then too that spiritual choices have to be made in total truth. No-one had said to me that my husband would die in two years. If they had, the choice would have been obvious. I had to make it for the right reasons myself. This is how it is always in spiritual law, we have to make the right choices for ourselves. Since that time I have no fear of death. The time preceding it perhaps; I fear suffering, but no longer the entry into a further expansion of life.

Some few weeks after this I was sitting again in the lounge with my husband, in front of an open fire. It was beautifully cosy and he fell into a deep sleep. I looked up and saw Sidney Richardson standing in front of me. He said: 'I want you to go and sit on the lavatory, your husband will not wake up.' He looked just as I was used to seeing him, in a white coat, very calm. I did as he asked, I didn't think about it until afterwards. Our 'loo' was separate but very small, but now there was plenty of space as though the walls had moved out. Sidney Richardson took my hands and two men, also in white coats, began to massage my back, the pain was quite dreadful. Sidney Richardson said: 'Come on, you've had worse pain that this, count slowly.' I got to six and I felt something dislodge through the rectum and fall into the pan. Everything vanished, I was alone and when I looked the water in the pan was absolutely clear, except for a tiny piece of bone, almost like a shaving, with a dark black spot in the middle. Why I didn't think to extract it I don't know. I was told later, through Ursula Roberts, it was a tiny piece of damaged vertebra that was pressing on a nerve and causing all the pain.

Now here is something to think about. If you look or read Estelle Roberts' book you will find a similar kind of case described, although in that case the piece of bone materialised into the medium's hand. Another strand of the tapestry joins here, out of context, because in the meantime there was also a connection between me and Estelle Roberts and I was aware of her guide Red Cloud. Here we have a coming together of two wonderful healing forces. From then onwards I had no more pain in that particular part of my back. Believe it or not as you will but it happened!

After that I began to feel physically much better and one day Sidney Richardson said his job was done and he wouldn't be coming any more. However, one night he did come, again with Ursula. She continued to come and talk to me as I had known it, the candle appearing in one corner of the room, intermittently, always with this lovely feeling of serenity. The red candle would appear first, in the corner and shortly afterwards I knew she was in the room, and I would be so glad to talk to her. On this one occasion she left slightly before Sidney Richardson appeared for the last time. He had just looked in, so to speak; I said to him that I would, when I was better, go to see Ursula and tell her about it all and take her some violets, because I had been told that she was very fond of them. He said, 'You will become a friend of my wife's but take her mixed spring flowers.' In the early spring of 1965 I did just that. Later I did become a friend of Ursula's, and know her to this day. I worked as one of her healers for two or three years, at the Spiritualist Association, and was privileged to study under her.

But that comes further ahead in my story.

To pick up the thread of my contact with Red Cloud. After I had broken the contact with the nun I continued to hear voices. I believed the voices I heard must be good and that because I was responding in true faith I would be protected at all times. I now understand that this is not necessarily so and if anything is told us which deeply offends our reason it is wise to reject it. I used to hear these voices during the aforementioned four months, very often, running concurrently with other experiences I have already described. They used, at the beginning, to intimate that if I had sufficient faith and did exactly as they said, it would be proved I would be one of the finest mediums etc. etc.

I imagined, first of all, that these instructions came from Chan because he was the only spirit teacher I knew. 'If you shut your eyes and walk across the road we will see you safe.' I did. Over a main road! I did this two or three times. I wanted to prove my complete trust. I could hear people shouting, yelling, cursing. At the third occasion it was as though something screamed inside me, 'Open your eyes,' I did, I was walking straight into an iron lamp post, I would have been very badly hurt. Then I heard a very gentle compassionate voice say, 'Don't you understand no-one like Chan would ask these things of you?'

Another time I insisted that my husband drove me in the middle of the night to a rendezvous. We were in bed and I insisted that he get up. I said another car would be coming from London and this would prove that I was not going out of my mind, and it would contain four people whom I named. Maurice Barbanell, probably because in those days I used to read *Psychic News* and looked forward very much to it, and Ralph Rossiter, Secretary of the S.A.G.B. I can't remember the other two. I absolutely insisted that this was arranged and I was picking it up mediumistically and it would happen. I was giving a running commentary and told my husband at which point they would be; the timing was about correct if a car had indeed left London at that time. I could hear the car getting nearer and nearer. Eventually it was almost at the point where we were. Then everything ceased and I heard a rather unpleasant laugh. It was quite dreadful.

This type of thing happened more than once. I realised that it was up to me not to obey, not to involve my husband and that I also needed help. Sometimes it was made very difficult for there was always a certain amount of truth in it. Thank God my husband was away often at that time. He was becoming very worried over me and how to deal with the situation. His work took him abroad for two or three weeks during the very worst period.

I was at work once and I was told 'You must go home, your mother is dead.' I did force myself to hang on until it was time to leave at 1 p.m. Then I ran as best I could, panting and terrified. I was nearly home when I heard, 'She won't be there, she's gone to your sister's to die.' I rushed indoors and found a note from my mother to say that she had indeed gone down to my sister for the day. There was always an element of truth in it all. Especially once I started to fight back.

It was then that I had a blinding flash to 'phone Estelle because I had a strange feeling that I was in touch with her mentally. This of course proved ridiculous on a conscious level. Anyway I rang her up. She was elderly then and lived at Hampton. In my total ignorance I imagined she would know why I had rung her. She answered the 'phone herself and I said, 'Mrs Roberts, do you know why I have rung?' Naturally she said 'No' and I dropped the 'phone. I heard a voice say: 'Try again, this time someone else will answer, make an appointment to see her.' I felt I just couldn't. After a while I regained courage and did. Someone else did answer and I made an appointment to see her.

From then onwards I began to fight back. Helped I now know by the compassionate and highly evolved influence of her guide, Red Cloud.

I was unable to keep the appointment. I was too ill I think. I also gave up my job, I couldn't cope with everything that was happening to me. I then wrote a letter to Estelle pouring out all sorts of things. For some inexplicable reason I also put in the name of a psychiatrist someone had given me, written on a separate piece of paper, and a business letter heading showing that my husband was a Director of the firm for whom he worked. There was no logical reason for this, I was not behaving rationally in any case. I sent the whole thing off. The next day I had a terrible feeling of guilt that certain things that I had said in the letter were detrimental to other people.

I can see very clearly now the deep seated psychological insecurities that surfaced at this time. Also the very dominant ego. My energies were so wholly centred on the self. Like attracts like at both the higher and lower levels. During the worst period this resulted in a painful inner isolation. I forced myself to act towards my family as they would expect, I had no emotional reaction whatever. I felt nothing, no-one could reach me.

Spiritually, we are told, we are never given more than we can bear. I sometimes still doubt this. Especially when listening to people pouring out their accounts of devastating unhappiness endured somehow, besides which my own suffering at this time seems puny. The positive aspect of this depressive time is that I know at first hand how it feels to be thus isolated. How impossible to respond to 'Snap out of it.'

I know that whether mentally ill or psychically disturbed what is being experienced is as real as everyday normality. I may not be able to help. It may not be within the capability of my teacher Nemerah, but of myself at the human level I can say, 'I know how you feel, I really do, I am so sorry.' That in itself may help a little.

From time to time I was aware of Red Cloud. I had never seen a picture of him in colour. Nor have I to this day. Then I saw clearly in colour, but contrary to the black and white pictures I had seen of him. I don't remember that he had a beard. I was conscious then of a large feathered headdress, bronze skin, a presence of command and strength, surrounded by wonderful colour. When I recapture the picture in my mind, it is always with a faint, soft red haze underneath and behind. Rather like a luminous mist, that would roll back and reveal other colours behind. But I digress.

About a week later there was a letter from Estelle. I opened it with such hope only to find a note enclosing my unopened letter saying that no longer was she able to deal with cases of obsession and in any case was moving to Bournemouth and had no time. I had told her over the 'phone that I was in a state of obsession. Her letter was full of kindness and generosity and warmth. As I said, from the time I 'phoned her I began to fight back.

I put my unopened letter in my desk in the living room, beneath my mother's room. For some reason I was terrified of opening it. As I said, I couldn't remember what I had written but I felt a fear of facing what I had written. I felt it would reveal terrible things in myself, that I would have to face things about myself I didn't want to. There it stayed gathering poison for about three weeks. I couldn't even go near the desk. It felt as though a Sword of Damocles hung above my head. Then one day my mother came down and said: 'What on earth were you doing at 4 o'clock in the morning, I heard you opening your desk?' 'Mother, I wasn't even in that room,' I answered. 'Oh yes you were, I heard you!' She obviously didn't believe me, so then I forced myself to go to the desk. There was Estelle's opened letter, there was my letter, still sealed, apparently completely untouched. Lying by the side of it was the business letter heading and the other piece of paper with the address of the psychiatrist! I remember my sense of complete disbelief. Turning the letter over and over in my hand, trying to find some evidence of it having been tampered with. There was none. Then I did open the letter and read it. There was nothing in it of which I needed to feel ashamed or have feared, or needed to fear. Influenced by some inner guidance, I suppose it still must have been Red Cloud at that time, I felt, or was told: 'Burn it, do not tear it up and throw it away, burn it,' which I did and felt freed. Many many years later, when I had begun to work with my own revered teacher Nemerah, who works often in helping people deal with fear, he always says there are exceptions to almost every rule but none in the case of 'A fear faced is a fear halved.'

I would like here to register my unfailing gratitude to the spirit teachers who call themselves Chan, Red Cloud, Ramadan and Nemerah, for their goodness, strength and wondrous compassion. I have never called on them without receiving help in abundance, love beyond measure.

However I did not then know my own spirit teachers but I suspect they were implicated and helped me on these occasions also. I used to feel my hand held and I used to draw. I did this once in front of my daughter and my husband. My hand went round and round, very very fast, drawing hundreds and hundreds of black circles, I used a pen and the actual picture was formed by the amount of paper left white. It was extraordinarily clever and beautiful. My daughter at the time said she would have liked to have taken it to school to show her Art Teacher. She, of course, as did my husband, believed I was doing it myself. I really could not have, nor can I. Actually it happened while writing to a psychic friend and the picture meant something to her. This never happens now, even if I try. Many extraordinary things happened at that time, which I have never been able to explain. Once I was writing some verses on some rather fine foolscap paper. I was reading it back to myself when the paper, and only the paper, was rained on. I was sitting indoors and water fell on the paper and the ink began to run. I was holding it in my right hand, a little away from myself, quite naturally as you would hold something to read, and it became soaking wet. It stopped. The paper dried out with the writing distorted and the paper crinkled. I kept it for quite a long time. There simply wasn't an explanation.

Another happened while I was still working. My employer liked a particular milk drink when we all had tea and coffee. I'd never heard of it and the secretary said there was only one place she could get it and she kept a supply for him. One afternoon I was in the Co-operative shop in Hillingdon, it was as though someone took hold of the back of my neck and said: 'Look!' Among the coffee, tea, Horlicks, Ovaltine etc. was just one jar of this drink – I can't remember its name. 'We've apported it for you,' I heard. So I took the jar, the price was stamped on it by the maker. When I paid for it, the woman behind the counter said: 'I've never seen that before, I didn't know we stocked it.' Next day I took the jar to work and was duly thanked for my thoughtfulness. So the next week I went and asked for the brand again. 'We don't keep it dear.' 'Oh yes I got it here last week.' The assistants got quite irate and called the manager who said in effect he hadn't heard of it, had never stocked it and I simply could not have got it there and I was mistaken.

Something of a similar nature happened some time afterwards, during the period I was training under Gordon Turner. I had three of my sister's small children staying with me. I was never a particularly good manager with money, and had given a friend, who was really in need, a pound. A pound went a great deal further in those days! In retrospect it sounds ridiculous but I really couldn't afford to do this from the amount of housekeeping money I had, without having to ask my husband for more. Normally this would have been no problem. In this particular case at this particular time, I knew he would not approve, because it was someone connected with me through the development circle. I took all five children into the park. My elder ones were playing with the little ones on the swings. I sat down on a bench nearby. I was worrying about this rather silly situation, when I had an odd tingling feeling down my spine. Impressed strongly into my mind came the words 'Look down, look down.' I looked down. I had my foot on a pound note. The bench was inset in concrete. It would have been impossible not to have seen the note had it been there previously. One of the little girls, suggested we should take it to the Police. I can't remember what I said but I didn't!

To continue with my narrative. Once I was in touch mentally with Red Cloud I began to understand that I, in some way, had to be in command of myself before I could hope to be of any positive use in the relationship with a higher intelligence. The attacks upon me physically stopped almost as soon as I had contacted Red Cloud or been contacted by him. The other phenomena continued in variety and I never knew at what time, or in what situation I would be subjected to them. I was wholly unable to control them. I became absorbed in them to the exclusion of the realisation of what I was doing, so that I would burn things that I was cooking, or suddenly find when in company that I had missed a whole exchange of conversation. Odd things would happen. I hold my bridge cards in a peculiar way. I still do, in reverse fashion to everyone else. It always causes amusement. One evening I was playing bridge and I felt my hand taken over and mentally heard someone say: 'For goodness sake don't hold them like that,' and the bridge cards were literally forced round and held in the way that everyone else holds them. That wasn't particularly unpleasant, it was only difficult to make it appear that I was doing it of my own volition. It was very strange to feel the currents running through me and to be subjected to this, while trying to keep up a conversation and appear normal.

Perhaps I should mention something that happened in between the death of my father and the time when I actually started to develop. We had a long-standing friend of the family called May. She had had a dreadful operation for cancer of the bowel and had been in hospital for some weeks. One night I found myself sitting up in bed. I knew that I had been awakened purposefully. Having had the one experience with my father I felt no fear. I heard a voice say 'Your help is needed, speak to May.' I then heard May's voice saying 'I can't see, I can't see!' I said: 'May, its Betty.' 'Oh Betty, oh Betty.' I felt her hand and held it, I was just about to say 'May, you are dead.' My head was seized as though in a vice. My thought forces were atrophied, I could neither see, speak nor hear. Very gently it was released. The voice said 'We didn't ask you to do anything except speak to her.' It was further explained that in the deeply depressive state in which she died, I was nearer to her than they were. They used a slower vibratory force in me before they would gently bring her to the understanding she had passed. 'We need your help, we did not want her shocked.' On rising the next morning I said to my husband: 'May died last night' and sure enough she had.

One day thinking about all this, I was reminded of a part of my life, during the war, when I was in the Air Force. I was a Radio Operator and worked at one time with 'homing' lost aircraft. When lost the aircraft emitted a radio signal on which a bearing was taken. This compass bearing relayed to the pilot would bring the plane back to base. It was also possible on the reciprocal to send the plane in exactly the opposite direction. The midpoint we called 'the point of no return'. This memory caused an instant reaction within myself. I understood that mediumistically I was 'a point of no return'. Once I accepted this I decided I would try to 'home' some of the spirit entities that I saw. The occurrences that followed were very strange indeed.

When we first came to live in the area there had been a public telephone box which no longer existed in its original postition. One day I saw clairvoyantly a man in this old telephone box, he was so real, I remember he had on grey flannel trousers and a jacket. He could see and hear me quite clearly also. In spite of my experience with May, I said boldly 'You're dead!' He started to bluster and became very frightened, swore and told me I was talking nonsense. 'Right,' I answered, 'This is my telephone number, 'phone me.' It was all so real. He felt in his pocket for twopence. He was trapped in time some way. He put the money in the box and nothing happened. Then he became very frightened indeed. He must perhaps have died in a 'phone box; I have no way of knowing. I asked him to say the Lord's Prayer with me. Again he blustered and swore. In the end his fright got the better of him and he did as I asked. I told him to continue saying the Lord's Prayer, at the same time to walk away from the sound of my voice. 'Walk away from it, someone will come to help you.'

I followed his progress. He walked a long long way, his voice becoming fainter and fainter. He was walking across open fields some of which I knew were built upon. I saw only fields shrouded in a grey mist. When I could barely hear him I saw what appeared to be a bank of quite heavy mist. As he came up to it, it began to roll towards him slightly. I heard very faintly, 'Its . . . its . . .,' there was a name, then with such relief 'Its my brother.' I stopped saying the Lord's Prayer. Immediately all was normal.

How long all this took I have no idea; or how many times I had said the Prayer. Sometimes I would look at the clock after such an event, and find I had taken two minutes, at others it would be an hour or more. Time just did not register. I always used the Lord's Prayer as my 'signal'.

Another time, I was in the kitchen having a cup of coffee. I was sitting on the Ideal boiler. It was quite safe to sit there. A man came into the kitchen. This time I could see him quite clearly right up to the point where he touched me or tried to touch me. As he came in I was more careful in my approach. I had dealt with several other cases by then. I said gently: 'You know you're not alive in the sense that I am, you're living somewhere else.' 'What nonsense, you're sitting on that thing over there.' I held out my hand to him saying 'Take my hand.' He came right up to me and our hands passed through each other. He was so real that I got up and opened the back-door for him which was quite ridiculous, I realise now. I can't remember what happened, I think he disappeared on that occasion after I opened the door. I never knew when these things were going to happen to me. I remember once it was in a cinema, right in the middle of a film, I used the same method, mentally, of sending out this note from myself and telling the entity to walk away from it. It was all very exhausting and sometimes I really didn't know how I was going to survive it.

There were some especially difficult experiences to face.

Again this one was at night. It happened fairly near the beginning. It is impossible for me to remember these things in sequence. I knew there was something awful to be faced in the corner of my bedroom. There was a space of about eighteen inches between the wardrobe and the wall. In some way a fear force had collected there. Fear itself is a force that creates its own magnetic energy. It creates a vortex into which anything of like nature is drawn. I didn't really know this at the time. I had read Estelle Roberts' book in which she speaks of a collective force of evil as a psychic rod. Collective fear has a similar effect. Alone one night I knew I must face it eventually. So when I was woken up, as usual about 3 a.m. I forced myself to get out of bed, go over to the corner and look into it.

Almost immediately this had become a pit that I was looking down into. It was very like the accepted version of Dante's Inferno. I was looking down, down, down and almost being drawn into a bottomless pit. The sides appeared rocky; curling from the sides and bottom were wisps of horrible sludgy greenish yellow mist. I can't remember how long I was looking into it when I heard a woman's voice: 'I'm in my coffin, I'm in my coffin.' 'No, you're not my dear,' I said. I leaned over, held out my hand, felt a hand in mine and pulled someone up. There was a sort of shudder and I was back in my bedroom. From then on there was nothing in that corner and never was again. I assumed then I had also lost contact with the nun – which in fact I had not, as I have previously explained.

One night I was getting changed to go out to dinner with my husband, I was doing my hair at the mirror and I was aware of a real force of malevolence coming up behind me, the worst sense of evil I have ever experienced. I don't like now to use that word evil. I recognised this power as coming from a man who had recently died. Instinctively I seized two

Victorian silver button-hooks that had been given to me by my mother, held them up in a shape of a cross in front of me and turned to face it. They flashed fire, I could see it, like lightning, flashing from the centre of the silver cross. A force of darkness was pushed from me and disappeared. After this I was not subjected to any more particularly baleful manifestation. From then onwards I made up my mind that I would not give way to the voices any more. Whether I heard them or not, I would not do what they told me. I did give way, once more, to these voices, far further on.

This was much nearer the ending of the whole initiation period, for that is how I now think of it. I was writing a letter when this voice told me that a friend I was particularly anxious to see and who had never been to the house, was trying to find it. I rushed upstairs where I could see the road, and sure enough there was a woman looking at the houses. From that distance she could well have been my friend. Her build, her way of walking were similar. I didn't run thinking she would eventually find the house. Coming downstairs I heard 'She is subject to fainting fits and has collapsed in the lane.' I said the Lord's Prayer and ran after her. The woman was then out of sight in a little lane that turned off the road. From the back view she still could have been my friend. She turned at hearing someone running behind her. It was a stranger. I made some silly excuse and came back to the house. I ran back in fact, crying and almost cursing the spirit world, hating it for allowing me to go all through this yet again. Panic stricken, in the kitchen I heard the compassionate voice I had heard once before, 'You could not walk to the end of the garden without losing your breath. Don't you realise you have run to the end of the road and back and you are breathing normally?' It was true.

I have dwelt at some length on the difficult and darker side of all that happened to me. There were also occasions of absolute beauty. Usually these happened when I was at rock bottom and felt that I couldn't go on. During the year or two before I had started to develop I had been involved in taking a friend to Harry Edwards' Healing Sanctuary, Burrows Lea, in Shere near Guildford. I saw some wonderful things happen there that I have never forgotten. During the same period I was writing to Harry Edwards for absent healing for someone else. When I took this particular friend, instead of posting my weekly letter I carried it with me and handed it to him. He was ageing then, quite portly in build. His eyes must once have been very blue. Rather faded by then, they were full of compassion as he accepted the letter. I looked into his eyes and there were no eyes; instead a brilliant golden light beyond. It was a type of shift, then I was looking once more into the kindly face of Harry Edwards.

One afternoon I had been ironing. It was a brilliantly sunny day and I had also started to write Christmas cards and amongst them was one to Shere. I looked out on to the garden, cold and crisp, in brilliant sunlight. The ironing board behind me was reflected in the window-pane. Then came another example of the pattern altering with the reflection, as had happened with the cretonnes and leather chair. The reflected top of the ironing board became the emblem used by the Sanctuary. A circle enclosing the cross. I knew I would get help from Burrows Lea. Taking the Christmas card I went out into the garden and stood there with the card between the palms of my hands. I had another experience of the flash of lightning. I thought of The Sanctuary with all my strength and my hands flashed fire again but this time it was in the opposite direction, the power flowed from outwards, through the sunlight in the brilliant garden into me and I was filled with strength and vitality.

Another time, after a particularly depressive stage, I was again looking out at the garden. There was quite a long lawn, the size of a tennis court. Beyond that there were four pine trees. Two tall ones in the middle and one smaller one each side. They divided the garden from a small plot of vegetables behind. Looking at these pine trees, feeling sad because I saw that there was a lecture by Chan on 'The Spirit of Christmas' I wanted so badly to go more than anything and I knew I couldn't; I knew I hadn't the strength or the ability to get on the train and make the journey. I so longed to go! I was aware of a clock and I noticed the time and it was about time for the lecture to begin. I looked out again on to the garden and there was descending upon the trees an enormous misty cloud. The cloud landed on the two trees and formed the figure of the Christ. I at no time thought of it as the Christ. I realised that it was a picture formation. The cloud gathered over the top of the two tall trees, above that was the head. I could see the beard, everything, in the pictorial figuration of Christ. There was such a feeling of strength, peace and love, I can't describe it. The mist stretched out and fell over the two smaller trees, like sleeves – and there was the whole enormous figure of the Christ which, while I watched, rose into the air. I could see it rising higher and higher and then passing very very gently over the house as though in blessing. I don't think I even thought of it as a blessing then but I was filled with love and serenity and peace; and in that time I heard and understood within my mind the whole meaning of the lecture. Then everything was back to normal and I was looking once more at the pine trees. My eyes went to the clock, the whole thing had taken exactly two minutes. I remembered this occasion very vividly many years later when I myself was invited to speak on 'The Spirit of Christmas'.

The next experience is extremely personal. I write about it in great detail because it meant and still means something for which I was and am, profoundly grateful. I loved my home and my house. It was a pretty house and I had realised that for a number of weeks I had given the family a hard time one way and another. A few days before Christmas I had been thinking that in all the years we had lived there I had never given a Christmas party. We always went away for Christmas and I had always wanted to give a Christmas party. The day before Christmas Eve I determined I would and told my husband that we were going to give a party on Boxing Night. It was very short notice, I hadn't planned anything and I looked at my far from shining house. I'd been too ill and wretched to do much housework. My husband was annoyed. He was tired and had had enough; he didn't want to be bothered, my mother didn't want it, she had had enough too. Our daughters were delighted! I was absolutely determined.

I then and there rang up friends. In all I asked about forty people and everyone I asked accepted. I invited complete families as well as young friends for the girls. If they had Grandma staying, then Grandma or Aunt was invited too. This was the day before Christmas Eve and our programme was settled. It meant that in order to do all this I had the afternoon of the 23rd, morning of the 24th, a tiny bit of Christmas morning plus the day itself. I like to write about this in detail because it was a party that was a wonderful success, exactly as I had planned and friends who came told me how much they had enjoyed it afterwards. For me it is a gift that remains with me through time. It was the last Christmas we were all together in the house, though of course I didn't know that then. The next one was a precious one. My husband and I were alone, the girls having gone to Israel and by Christmas 1966 he had died. This year he had been in Holland and then in South Africa and had been involved in a great deal of work and a lot of entertaining, almost up to Christmas. He was very tired and the last thing he wanted was a party at home; but I would brook no opposition. That in itself was out of character. So in fact it was the last Christmas we were all together in that house and I have my strange and lovely party to think about.

To get it all done I had to stay up almost all of Christmas Eve night. I planned the menu and made it simple. I had to start then and there by going to get it all. My daughters threw themselves into it. My elder daughter chivvied her father into taking the door between breakfast and dining room off to facilitate dancing. They made shining moons and stars to stick in all the window-panes, dozens and dozens of them. We had about thirty-six in each room I think. I rushed off to the shops with a push basket. On the way there I was assailed by the familiar dreadful feeling of weakness. I went on somehow and did all the shopping but when I was in the butcher's I realised that I was quite incapable of lifting the enormous turkey that I had bought into the basket. The butcher put it on the counter and I couldn't lift it. I felt very very ill. I heard a voice behind me saying 'When she turns round put your hand on it.' The woman at the till took my money and turned her head, I put my hand on the turkey and it lifted itself off the counter into my basket. I only had one hand on the side of it. I did what remained in a daze. On the way home I was told that the kind of phenomena I was experiencing wouldn't be possible soon but I knew I'd get help all through that Christmas and I did.

I don't want to keep repeating how ill I felt. I'd utterly exhausted myself physically and mentally. I was no longer in pain but these experiences had been going on for nearly three months day and night. I was near the end of my endurance mentally and physically. However, I made up my mind that come what may I would not spoil the Christmas for my family. When I got back, I don't remember how I managed to lift things out of the basket but I seemed to be able to do everything I wanted to do. My daughters threw themselves into helping wholeheartedly. Not so my husband. My mother retired to her room, refusing to have anything to do with it. My husband, coaxed by the girls, did what was asked of him very reluctantly. I decided that a lot of the furniture had to be moved, the rugs and carpets taken up, floors polished for dancing, it meant a great deal of work. The girls were a wonderful help but they wouldn't be there next day and I knew I must get on with it. I stayed up nearly all night.

I cleaned windows and put candles in bottles in the room for dancing, I made huge Christmas decorations by painting bare branches white. I painted leaves silver and gold, sprinkling them with glitter. I did an enormous arrangement of bare twigs, some of them painted white, some bare with silver and gold leaves and coloured balls. I moved so quickly. Extraordinary things happened. I stayed up three nights and I can't remember the episodes in sequence, only that they all happened during these nights. I looked at the kitchen fioor. It was dirty and needed scrubbing. I thought: 'I can't scrub it, I just can't.' I heard a voice say: 'Come on, enjoy it' and I became an enormously powerful woman. I put the mop in hot water and in five minutes that floor was clean. I was conscious of nothing, not even movement, I held the mop, that's all. It went with the speed of an automatic polisher. 'There,' she said, and I was myself again. I went up to the bathroom. There was one corner that was extremely difficult to get at. To clean it I had to stand on the bath in order to reach. I hadn't for weeks been able to risk standing across the bath in case I fell. This corner was by now extremely dirty. I looked at it hopelessly but I knew too that I wouldn't like guests seeing my house like that. In all probability they would not have noticed in any case! Someone said: 'Don't worry, we'll hold you but don't straddle the bath, put both feet on the side.' It was this practical command that fascinated me. 'Don't straddle the bath, put both feet on the side and lean across.' As I put my foot on the side of the bath somebody heaved me up and as I cleaned the wall I could feel two strong hands supporting my back, absolutely warm and firm.

I had always been childishly afraid of the dark; I liked to

make sure the coal buckets were filled during daylight for instance. If necessity demanded I always faced the dark. I don't think the family were even aware that I had the problem. At about 2 a.m. one morning, my Christmas decorations were completed except for one arrangement, I needed just one branch if I was to finish before I went to bed. I must go into the garden and get it.

It was a beautiful clear crisp night, cold with brittle starlight and the garden full of shadows. I was very fearful at the thought of leaving the security of the house. It was not essential. I recalled some of the terrifying things that had happened to me previously. However, taking a deep breath I went out into the night. I was picking what I wanted from the hedge when I heard a child crying. I found a little coloured spirit boy, about two or thereabouts. He could walk but he was very small. I held the branches with one hand and taking his hand with the other I led him into the kitchen. He stopped crying as we came indoors. Along one wall of the kitchen there was a long working top with fitted cupboards underneath. My unfinished vase was standing there. I lifted the child up to sit beside it. This time I couldn't see him with my physical eyes, only my inner eye. I could feel him absolutely solid and his weight as I lifted him. He was comforted and liked the coloured balls, watching me as I tied them on. Then without warning I felt a rush of warmth, there was a flash of light and he was gone. Within me came an inner lightening of my heart and I have never been afraid of the dark since. On Boxing Night by the time we awaited our first guests my husband was at his best; he was always a wonderful host. We called our house *Talawakelle*. All the rooms led into each other and the stairs led up from the breakfast room. It was decorated, shining and beautiful. Sofas and chairs pushed round the edge for as many to sit as possible. It was lighted throughout with candles and the table looked delightful. I popped in to see my daughters dressing, they looked gorgeous. It all sparkled and shone, all the curtains were drawn back. I loved the rooms because there were windows at both ends overlooking the garden back and front. A long table was placed in front of the window. It was set with a snow-white tablecloth and really a very simple central decoration. A huge wooden bowl piled really high with bright green apples. I'd rubbed them all individually with a cloth until each one gleamed. In between I had pushed sprigs of holly that had been painted gold and had set two candles on the table either side. The food too was simple but very nice. I walked through and I was so proud of it all. The flickering lights of the candles were reflected in the windows. Each pane twinkled with stars, earth and planets. The lovely arrangements of gold and silver leaves shimmered. The roaring open fire, the red brick polished fireplaces welcomed. Everything looked as I had hoped it would. Inside, warmth, gentle glittering light and colour, outside cold clear bright moonlight and stars.

People began to arrive and as we greeted them, I had to make the most determined effort to appear normal. I felt near to death with tiredness; worse, all through the evening I had heard and was hearing the voices. On this occasion, I was told that Estelle Roberts would arrive, as an unexpected guest. By now I knew it was unlikely to be true. However, I had an overwhelming hope that in some way something tangible would be given to me as proof that what I was going through was real. Of course it did not happen. I looked about me, and wondered what it was all about. My mother looked charming and as usual on such occasions was a wonderful help. For once there were people of her generation to talk to and she had a lovely time and I was glad for that. There was dancing, and all the happy things that go to make a party. Friends arrived at 7 o'clock and the last guests left at 4 or 5 a.m. in the morning. I was left with a sense of sadness, a foreboding that things would never be the same again, and yet with a sense of achievement. It was a kind of milestone. I have the knowledge now that it was also a spiritual gift. A gift that is magical as was my childhood. It grows and expands with understanding and love with the passing years. That is a spiritual gift. Such wondrous gifts of the spirit are within us all, inherent in the heart. They are as precious jewels hidden, their beauty unseen until illumined by the light of our growth.

It is with some difficulty that I face trying to write about the most powerful and awe inspiring spiritual experience of them all. I have never spoken about this from a platform. I have mentioned it sometimes to friends but with no effort to explain in detail how it took place. This is the first time I have tried to express it. I was again on my own. Thinking actively about my life past and present, I was full of self pity, dwelling particularly on the events I was caught up in which were so harrowing. Why should they happen to me? What had I done? I re-lived, or re-thought, parts of my life, always with the central figure of myself cast as the heroine. Concentrating on the wrongs I had suffered at the hands of others, I had then started to think about myself and my relationships with those closest to me whom I loved so dearly. I felt that in some respects they had failed and were still failing me. From high above I heard a voice of thunder. I will never forget it, for it *was* a voice of thunder. 'Look again!' I went step by step through scenes of my life. I can remember things that happened long before I could walk or talk. The earliest recollection I have, is of being taken to the beach by my ayah. There she met several of her friends all with their small charges. The ayahs would sit in a line, their backs against a sea wall. They sat with outstretched legs. At their feet would be placed an open umbrella and we would crawl about in the shadows thus made. I would crawl determinedly over the outstretched legs always to be frustrated in my efforts to get to the sea. The ayah at the end would always pull me back and turn me round towards my own nurse. The scene is so vividly in my mind, so bright with colour. My mother confirmed this was true and said at the most I could have been nine months old.

So I re-traced my life, recognising as I did so, the defects and blemishes in my character, that showed in my behaviour as a child and were still apparent in me now. I didn't actually hear the voice again but the whole of my life unfolded in memory with a different vision. I saw the falsifications and how the negations within myself brought about the very situations that I had so resented. How often I had twisted events in my own mind in self-justification. How I dwelt so consistently on the wounds inflicted upon me, with no regard for the wounds I had inflicted on others. It was the most shattering and devastating entry into the realms of truth.

During this occurrence, after the initial shock of hearing the voice, I was still connected in some way with a very powerful mind energy. In trying to recapture it I find it almost impossible to describe. It was as though I was unconfined by a building of any kind. A total awareness of light and space. In this case a registration of powerful intelligence which in no way was judging me. In no way could I release myself from the hold of that mind. I was not being judged but I was subjected to a trial by myself of myself, that is the only way I can describe it. It was, I think now in retrospect, an understanding of what hell truly means. Because I had had the near death experience, and everything that I had undergone had been of the mind, this was in keeping with that part of it. If I had died, I believe I would have had to go through exactly the same experience in some other place. I believe that we all have to do this when we leave this part of our existence. I believe we create our own heaven and our own hell. This is hell and I think no-one can do it for us, we have to do it ourselves. This is a conclusion that I have reached afterwards of course. At the time it was just a realisation of that which in myself allowed it to happen.

I had to face that like attracts like, if those things happened to me it was because there was that darkness within myself that allowed it. I saw these areas acutely and clearly; there was no way I could hide from myself. It is a bitter thing to face and causes much anguish; it is a process of soul evaluation. Mercifully that which is of truth and love is also clearly seen.

Though I remember quite clearly some of what happened to me during this period it is too complicated to relate. Over the years I think I have come to understand most of it. The mind is a delicate instrument. At that time I was functioning at several levels concurrently with no safety doors between.

I had no understanding of the mechanism that governs the psychic body, or of the powerful energies that can be released. Deeply emotional, I had no knowledge of the insecurities that lay within myself or the depth of my own fear. I had no acceptance of my own inadequacies and no realisations of my own self-centredness.

I had reached an altered state of consciousness which had opened for me doors to mental and spiritual horizons up to then tightly closed. It was as though I stood in a maze, its convoluted paths leading to a centre which I knew was there and must find. The paths themselves were lighted but overgrown with tangled bushes. Overriding all was fear.

I did not know then that I was at the beginning of a wonderful period of exploration in the 'Unfolding Journey' of my life. I did not know then of my coming partnership with my own teacher Nemerah: or that the very nature of my own negativity and darkness would be a cornerstone on which he would build. For when I was ready to be his instrument, he talked often of fear. He teaches of its crippling effects, above all of our own ability to free ourselves from its domination.

About the beginning of February I decided it was time to return to development class. I found the prospect daunting. It took quite a lot of moral courage. I imagined everyone would look at me and remember that I was the woman who had made such a fool of herself. I had centred so wholly on myself during this period I had forgotten that for others I was a passing episode in the living of their lives.

However, having made the decision, one afternoon I set off for Belgrave Square. Just before I reached the building I was very much aware of the closeness of my spirit friends. Once more I have to stress the infinite love of the spirit people, so compassionate in their understanding of my need and in their care of me. They closed in on me. I felt as though I was surrounded by three or four people, tightly packed around me. They took me straight up to the healing floor. I saw nobody I knew. I was still weak and found it difficult to walk up all those stairs. On reaching the top I saw Albert Denton. I went straight up to him and said: 'Mr Denton I'm your nun.' He looked at me blankly and I reminded him. He of course didn't understand about the nun; how could he? He did recall the occasion and when I thanked him he patted me on the back, in exactly the same way that I had seen him do to others; called me 'friend' and said: 'It's wonderful to see you well, this is what makes our work so worth while.' The memory of his kindness is still with me. On coming downstairs again I saw members of the class in the entrance hall. They had their backs to me so didn't see me. 'Out, it is enough' I was told. I went quickly through the door and home.

I started then to go back once a week. I cannot begin to express the kind of gentle care with which I was guided at this time. It is difficult to explain how intensely vulnerable I felt, as though I had a skin less. People hurt me terribly. They didn't intend it but they had been frightened by what had happened. Speaking to me in passing they would move away as quickly as possible. If I sat next to someone awaiting a lecture, after a moment or two they would make an excuse and change their place. It was a perfectly understandable reaction that I found, at the time, difficult to cope with. They felt, I think, that they didn't want to be involved. For me it was an intensely emotional period, governed on the one hand by my extreme sensitivity and on the other by my increasing attunement with the inter-change of spirit. I was cushioned by their presence, which was withdrawn very very gradually, until I myself could accept the situation in my own right.

I made an appointment to see Ursula Roberts at her home in Hendon. I took her the flowers that I had promised Sidney Richardson I would. At the beginning of the interview she asked me if I would like a trance sitting. I felt at the time that was the last thing I wanted. I wished to be in touch with ordinary people at all levels. I asked her if she would be prepared just to listen to me. I told her in detail everything that had happened. It seemed to take a long time. She listened quietly, when I had finished she said: 'What do you want from me?' 'Just that you believe that it is true.' 'Of course I believe you,' she answered, 'I believe every word of it.' The overwhelming sense of relief that her words brought was a healing in itself. She went on to say that if I wished to continue my development, she would be prepared to help me. If that was so, I should come and see her again in three or four months time. So many people to thank. Sidney Richardson and Ursula Roberts stand very high on the list.

Though I was very grateful of the help I had received, I was still sure in my own mind that my path lay with the type of teaching that was offered by Chan and Ivy Northage. Mrs Northage still felt that I was not ready to return to class. From where I stand now I know she was absolutely right. Then it didn't seem so, I felt rejected and hurt.

One day, after yet another refusal on her part, I was coming down the stairs when I saw below me Gordon

Turner. He was standing at the reception desk, exactly as I had seen him all those months before. I remembered my talk with him in the middle of the night. Without hesitation, I ran down the stairs, went straight up to him; we had never actually met in the flesh of course. 'Mr Turner, my name is Elizabeth Farrell, will you take me for healing classes please?' He looked upwards over my head, for a second or two, smiled, 'Yes.' The receptionist began to remonstrate. 'Your class is full Mr Turner, you have a waiting list.' He cut her short, 'Turn somebody out, or put an extra one in. She's in, I insist!' With a wave of his hand and another smile he was gone.

Shortly after this I began classes with him. It was heart-warming to become part of a group again. I was with him for about six months I suppose. He was at times unreliable and sometimes wouldn't come for several weeks without letting us know. We learned though a lot about generosity and compassion from him. He was a wonderful healer, passionately fond of animals, above all extremely kind. He was then very well known. The demands on his time and energy must have been harrowing. When he was with us he gave no sign of this.

He was very practical in his approach as a teacher. He knew a lot about anatomy and the general working of the human body. He never allowed us to become too intense. He would bring us down to earth with a graphic mime of a 'would be healer' or tell us a funny story, often at his own expense, resulting in all-round laughter.

He explained something that had always intrigued me. That was the necessity of showmanship and the shop window. If you are to interest people in something you have to offer, then at times you must demonstrate that you have something worthwhile, that the big platform demonstrations of healing had a place. For this, instant reactions to the healing were very important. Therefore people selected as examples and chosen from the audience would often be such cases. The healing would have been spectacular in public or in private. Sometimes the demonstrator would recognise this from the platform himself, or it would be organised by spirit intervention. Obviously those capable of producing spectacular results in public are comparatively rare. After all there are not too many worldwide acknowledged pianists, dancers or singers. The collective power of a large gathering is also a factor.

Through reading, talking with others, and the training I was undergoing with Gordon Turner, I came to understand in some degree what had happened to me. I came to accept that we have a psychic body co-existent with our physical and that the psychic body is 'fed' with energy through the psychic centres or as they are usually known chakras. These centres are protected by a natural insulating web which allows into the centres exactly the psychic energy appropriate to the whole being; that is, of our combined development, spiritual, psychic, mental and physical. If this remains in balance all is well. We interfere with it, and this web gets broken or torn.

This happens under drugs, excessive alcoholism, or under deep emotional shock, which is what had happened to me. A torn aura mends usually with disciplined help of healers and with the discipline of the person concerned.

Here of course I was in an ideal situation. I was in a controlled class under an expert healer. We always began class with a protective prayer and we systematically closed our psychic centres at the end of a session. We usually then had tea together, often joined by Gordon, which thoroughly 'grounded' us. For my part I found the strength to refuse absolutely any conscious reaction to the voices.

Gradually unasked-for infiltration of any sort stopped. I felt once again able to ask if I could go back to training with Ivy Northage. To my great joy I was accepted back to class with her in May of 1965. For a little while there was an overlap of the two classes. Then we were told that our healing class must come to an end. What I learned from Gordon has remained invaluable to this day.

Beginning classes again I had to face quite a different challenge. I expected that because of the immediate ability I had had to see and hear, clairvoyantly and clairaudiently in the state of obsession, these faculties would return very quickly under development. What I had not realised, and it took me quite a while to accept and understand, was that I had been ill and etherically loose from my body. Now I was well and strong and I was therefore not in this state. I had also to come to terms with another important factor. In terms of mediumship, I believe, there are first and second class citizens. I think that the first class citizens are those who are completely natural mediums and have the gift from birth, and the second class citizens are those who have above average psychism but must train to make it viable, thus achieving mediumship.

I began by going to class once a week. In those days The Ivy Northage School of Mediumship wasn't in existence. Instead Mrs Northage used to give small pupil demonstrations to an invited audience. She chose a chairman, and other pupils would demonstrate various aspects of our training. There was one such occasion fairly soon after I joined the class. We had been told that in case we should be chosen as chairman we could formulate a chairman's speech. I returned home and told my mother that there would be one of these demonstrations. She said instantly, 'You'll be chairman.' My mother was extremely psychic in her own way, in fact in my family I'm surrounded by people who are more naturally psychic than myself. Anyhow, at this time, she insisted that she should hear my speech. She then trained me during that week. She made me stand at one end of the house, she at the other with the doors open between. Unless she could hear every word, from beginning to end, she would not accept my work. She proved to be right. As a result of her training and the subsequent small demonstrations, I had the chance to act as Chairman at the S.A.G.B. itself for public demonstrations of clairvoyance. I couldn't have had a better training. In those days the standard of mediumship was very high indeed. I was privileged to chair for some wonderful mediums and to see demonstrations of clairvoyance that were excellent and not by just one medium but by many.

Mrs Northage herself was completely professional in her approach. She would say to us; make the best of yourself and then forget yourself. I used those very terms later on when I had my own students, in fact I still do. I was very happy at that time. I thoroughly enjoyed going to class, I looked forward to it every week. My husband was still rather against it and made things very difficult for me, in the nicest possible way. He would ring up on a Tuesday to say that he had tickets for the theatre, or Centre Court Wimbledon tickets, something very special that he had got just for us. Sometimes I would miss class and sometimes I would suggest he took my elder daughter in my place, if that was possible. Certainly if it was to the Opera; I wasn't very keen on opera in any case. It was more difficult when it was my duty to be with him entertaining other executives, especially if he had lovely tickets to the Ballet at Covent Garden. These things always seemed to happen on a Tuesday! There was at that time a school of thought, and still is I believe, of total dedication toward class. Class came first. I didn't always find it possible to agree with this. I wanted to go to class first but I also felt that I had a responsibility that I had accepted as a wife and that responsibility also should be respected. So occasionally there were difficult decisions to make.

When the girls were home from school, we made a habit of going out together as a family either on Saturday or Sunday evening. One Sunday evening we were just leaving at about six o'clock when I had a sudden premonition that I was needed at the little Spiritualist church in Hillingdon, formerly a small church hall. It had been my salvation during the time of my obsession. I had gone there for solace and nearly always received a message of hope and encouragement. For instance, once I had received a message.'In three weeks time you will be among friends.' Three weeks later I had been accepted by Gordon Turner. Another occasion remains vividly in my mind, particularly at the present time. The medium came from Birmingham and was an excellent trance medium. I quote something that was given while in trance as nearly as I can remember: 'In the lifetime of many of you here at present, the existence of the spirit world will be proved, not by the Spiritualist, but by the scientists.' On this particular Sunday I turned to my family and asked that they please go without me, I felt I must go to Church. My husband was not best pleased, but he agreed and dropped me at this little church. I wondered why, or if indeed, I really had had this call. I can't remember the name of the medium, she was very good indeed. She had a slightly cockney accent which disappeared completely once she started to give the prayer. I realised she was speaking inspirationally and that she was under control. The address was beautiful. I was sitting in the middle of the church having taken the last chair on the centre aisle. When the time came for the clairvoyance, she got up, looked round the church and said: 'Ah, there she is', and, looking straight at me, she continued: 'My best friend died yesterday and although I know she's alright I myself have not enough power to do the clairvoyance without help. I was told my power point would be here.' She walked down the aisle and put her hand on my shoulder. I felt the power flowing through me into her, while she stood there and gave the clairvoyance from the centre of the church.

Initially my development went fairly well. In those days Mrs Northage used to take her more advanced pupils with her to morning services. They would take the platform with her either doing the clairvoyance or the address under her watchful eye. It was an ordeal, nevertheless a unique opportunity to learn.

It was a particularly beautiful summer. I recall many happy family occasions. My husband had taken to growing carnations. As a beginner he was surprisingly successful. He had planted a bed of these carnations outside the breakfast room window. They were of every variety in colour and very beautiful. We could also look down on them from our bedroom window above. He was extremely proud of them. The very first thing he did when he got up in the morning was to look out at his carnations. On September 10th he went to play in an all day cricket match.

We were expecting him home to supper, I looked out on to the garden, and the exquisite bed of carnations. They were in full bloom, and I realised that unless I gathered some of them at once, it could be too late to pick any. So I picked some of the loveliest blooms, and began arranging them in a bowl, conscious of the spicy aromatic scent. I looked at my watch to check the time. It was a quarter to seven. He did not return at the expected time. Later on that evening they came to tell us he had collapsed on the cricket field, and died on the way to the hospital at about a quarter to seven.

It was an appalling shock to us all. Later during the remnants of that awful night, I accepted that part of me had always known it would be so. He had told me before we were married, that whilst in the Army during the war, and in the desert, an Arab had 'drawn his future in the sand', telling him he would die before he was forty. A splinter of fear went through my heart, and I asked him if he believed it. He laughed and said he didn't. He forgot about it completely as far as I know. He certainly had many ideas planned for the future.

When he reached the age of thirty-nine I worried about it

inwardly a great deal but did not remind him. When he had his forty-second birthday I too decided it was nonsense and pushed my fear from me. He was forty-six when he died.

Two or three weeks previously I had been watching my elder daughter and her father painting her pony's stable. It was a glorious day, full of laughter and happiness. I had a feeling of sudden panic over my personal situation. The mediumistic side of my life was becoming more and more important to me. At the same time I could see that my part in our social life together was likely to increase also. My family and our life together was precious. I knew I would have to make a choice.

I took myself to a nearby meadow in some distress. Sitting quietly I had called on my spirit friends and asked 'How shall I manage?' The response came with immeasurable love and compassion: 'You will not have to make a choice.' I went back to watching the painting, joined in the laughter and badinage, carefree and happy. Somehow it would it be alright. It never occurred to me that my husband would die, neither did I recall the prophecy. Staring into the darkness, trying to assess some of the immediate effects his death would have on us, I remembered.

I recalled scene after scene of our life together. At that time I could make no judgement. It was rather like watching an inward film. He was born under Gemini. Quiet and unassuming to meet he had a will of iron. Living with him I had learned a little about kindness for kindness sake, of helping with no thought of recognition, or indeed any thought that there should be. He would go to incredible lengths to help people if he could in any possible way – passers-by, friends, acquaintances. He was an animal lover and had a wonderful sense of humour.

He hated pretence of any kind and had complete integrity. He was a perfectionist. Every task, large or small, that he undertook had to be done as perfectly as possible for the sake of quality. He thought and moved three times as quickly as anybody else. Our lives revolved around him.

In the home he was very unselfish as to our pleasure, when he was there. He threw himself whole-heartedly behind our daughters' main interest; horses in one case, ballet in the other. On the other hand he would not allow us a television while the girls were young. We had one only about a year before he died. I now think he was right about that also. At the time I resented it.

Of course he had his faults, as we all have. Living with a perfectionist is difficult in itself. When it came to home decorating, how I sometimes longed for less perfection and a job completed. Uncompromising himself, he could be unbending and found emotionalism difficult to cope with. Rational and logical at most times, when he lost his temper he was impossible and sometimes very unfair. Luckily this didn't happen often.

He carried heavy responsibilities and worked sixteen to eighteen hours a day, often bringing work home with him and working into the night. This meant that the decisions over the children were made by me, but he always supported me. When he was in the family circle, he threw off all care, throwing himself completely into whatever we were doing. Always with jest, merriment and laughter. He packed his life full measure and gave wholly of himself with true generosity, his time, his talent and his vitality.

I thought of how many people loved him. We had an elderly baby sitter. She was very badly off and lived in rather a run down area. She used to say my husband was the only person who, when he drove her home, opened the car door, handed her out and saw her safely into her home before he left. She thought highly of him for this. I knew it would not have occurred to him to do otherwise.

I thought of the elderly neighbour, also badly off, who had

come in one day while he was there and mentioned that she used to translate books for her father.

Several weeks afterwards, he came home, and had arranged through connections with his firm for some work for her, which she could do at home. This meant that he had to remember to collect and deliver it. She was so delighted. I wondered how many men in his position would have bothered.

Lying in the dark I thought of many such instances in our life together. I thought too of his once saying to me 'If I believed in any religion I would be a Buddhist.' We were almost exact opposites, but had achieved over the years understanding, tolerance and friendship. I knew somewhere he was alive still, that he loved us and would know I knew it also. In some way sooner or later he would contact me. I knew he was my friend for always. It didn't take away my sense of loss, my sorrow, or my fear of facing life alone. The next day and the days after came telegrams, letters, phone calls. The first telegram I opened read 'He was the finest man I've ever met.' What a lovely epitaph.

Because of my husband's love of carnations we chose these flowers to be placed on his coffin.

Since then I have had the most extraordinarily tender and beautiful occurrences which involved carnations. I think back on them with joy. They have happened intermittently over many years and is yet another gift from spirit. Some time later my sister, who is extremely clairvoyant, was visited by an Avon lady who was selling her skin perfumes. She became aware of my husband. Her clairvoyance is objective and she could see him quite clearly standing behind the saleswoman. She looked at the flower perfumes that were being shown her and heard my husband say: 'Ask her for the one in her handbag she hasn't shown you.' My sister looking at them, rather diffidently asked if she had any others. The woman answered that there was one coming on the market but she only had a sample with her which was not yet fully packaged. She took from her handbag a little pot of skin perfume and on the lid there were coloured drawings of carnations. My husband said: 'Please buy it and give it to Elizabeth with my love. I cannot repay you in money but I will repay you in kind when I can.' My sister bought the perfume for me. I still have the jar. So carnations have come to mean a sign between us of continued thought and care. This sign has been given me over and over again. Not so often now but frequently after his passing. People would come to me and hand me one, two, sometimes a spray or a bouquet of carnations. They would say, that on the way to see me, they had felt impelled to buy them. If I was particularly nervous of an occasion always I would receive, from some source or other, carnations. This has happened time after time after time.

One example that I love to recall happened many years after his death. My daughter, who lives in South Africa, was bringing her baby girl to England for the first time. The whole family went to the airport to meet them. We came back to my flat and on the doorstep was a magnificent bouquet of carnations. It was a moment of complete joy. I knew that once more my husband had joined us in thought on a very happy occasion.

The flowers had been sent me from a Church that I had served the week before. When I rang the President of the Church to thank her, she was quite annoyed. She had been promised that they would be delivered the previous Tuesday.

I have come to understand how such precision in timing is achieved. In the particular instance quoted, a positive action was already in progress. No-one would be hurt by an alteration in sequence. So a strong thought force would have resulted in perhaps an order being mislaid or misread. For me to be presented with carnations, the communicator is dependent upon a recipient who is both psychic at an intuitive level and generous of heart. People coming to see me professionally often have these qualities.

On one birthday, a professional artist who is herself very psychic, made for me a charming hand painted card. She chose to paint a red carnation! In her work she hides an emblem as her signature. Starting to paint in this emblem, hidden in a tendril of a leaf, she felt impelled to turn this instead into the letter E. In writing to tell me of this, she assumed that for some reason someone had wanted my initial to appear in the painting. My husband has the same initial. I use this card still, as a marker in my desk diary. These personal assurances do not happen so frequently now, partly I think, because I know so positively that my husband can reach me when he wishes so to do. Also because this particular way of linking has become known, and therefore more difficult to achieve with spontaneity.

The most wonderful example of spirit manipulation and stage management happened at the marriage of my younger daughter. It is her story. I tell it with her permission.

It was a July wedding and a glorious summer day. Rehearsal two days previously with choir, organist, bridesmaids, had gone without a hitch. We all knew exactly at what moment we should move. My daughter came up the aisle on the arm of a family friend, followed by her sister as chief bridesmaid and young friends who had grown up with her. I sensed my husband's presence, remembering my own wedding in the same church, I mentally registered to him 'She looks beautiful doesn't she?' I knew he would receive my thought.

The service proceeded towards the end, when the Vicar unaccountably altered slightly the agreed procedure. This resulted in my friend and myself moving too quickly towards the chancel steps. We realised the error immediately and stood still. This meant that I was directly in line with my daughter unimpeded by anyone else, as bride and groom were led up to the altar for the blessing. We were then asked to join in two minutes of silent prayer for their well-being. Obviously I opened up both psychically and from the heart sending my full power towards them. My daughter turned round and gave, as I thought to me, a smile of the utmost radiance. An elderly friend commented later 'What a lovely lovely smile, but she had no business turning round!'

While waiting for guests to arrive at the reception my daughter told me that she had felt someone coming up behind her where she knew no-one else should be. To quote her:

> I quickly glanced round, Daddy was standing to my left but behind me, where he would have been had he been giving me away. He was in full morning dress – but funnily enough had his topper on. Then of course I had to face front. I'm not sure when he went. I am sure he was there throughout the service, but I don't remember being aware of him when we went into the vestry to sign the Register.

PART THREE

A WORKING LIFE IN MEDIUMSHIP

It was just a week after my husband's death that I took my place on the platform as Mrs Northage's pupil speaker. I was much praised for this at the time but in truth it would have been more difficult not to have done so. It seemed an affirmation of faith. Also I was surrounded by light and aware of an inner quality of unbounded love which supported me completely. It was there for about two or three weeks and after that slowly dissipated. Then came my real test or trial. Things were much more difficult to face. If I had had to make that speech three weeks later I am not sure if my reaction would have been the same.

Obviously the life pattern changed. We moved to the Richmond area and I threw myself whole-heartedly into psychic development, attending class two or three times a week. Under Mrs Northage's tuition my ability as a speaker increased and within a year or so I was being asked in my own right to speak in the Spiritualist Churches, when they required both speaker and clairvoyant.

Unfortunately the level of my clairvoyance did not reach that of my ability as an inspirational speaker. Work as I did, try as I would, I could not find the key to unlock the clairvoyant eye. I decided that in some way I would have to explore a further avenue of teaching. I left Ivy Northage, with her approval, and went to Ursula Roberts. Her approach was different and perhaps at that time was the correct one for me.

I began in a class known as 'The Inspirational Class'. In this class we were asked 'What do you feel inspired to do?' and then encouraged to try. I said that I would like to attempt flower clairsentience. This is a lovely thing to do. It is very difficult to teach anybody how, unless they have a feel for it. Ursula very quickly established that I had an instinctive aptitude towards this gift. When I did it first, she asked if it really was the first time I had attempted it. I assured her it was. Ursula increased my self-confidence immeasurably by inviting a group of people, unknown to me, at a practice demonstration, and then recommending me to others.

From then on I began to do flower clairsentience professionally, and was invited to do demonstrations at many of the churches I already served as a speaker. I would usually take a group of six to eight people. I think it was the fact of being accepted professionally in two aspects of work which gradually built up the inner security I needed to continue my attempt to regain clairvoyance. My confidence had been very shattered. I had not realised that I would be unable to 'see' in the way I could during my initiation period.

The next step was very much Ursula's recognition that I was a potential trance-medium and she brought this through, again in a wonderfully secure way for me. She just put me upstairs in a tiny room by myself with two of her dedicated healers and they taped every word I said. They transcribed the tapes, which both Ursula and I read. In this way my trance-mediumship began to develop. I was very worried again because the first control I had was a nun. She was a French nun and her name was Elizabeth, I wouldn't accept this at all because the name was the same as mine. 'This has to be another part of myself' I thought, until one day she very quietly questioned, 'Is there no-one in your world also called

Elizabeth?' After that I went along with it more definitely. We then reached a healing guide called Saphros. Saphros gave me a lovely feeling of attunement because I could actually see him. I did not ever see him in front of me but I was always able to see him behind me. It seems extraordinary but I could, I could see him quite clearly, he was quite a portly man and wearing a long white robe. I don't ever remember seeing his face absolutely clearly but I was very aware of him when I was healing. It was a very close alliance that he brought, and people loved him.

There was one rather interesting transcript that remains and it seems appropriate here. It is dated 1st October, 1968. Saphros was asked if he would say something of the mechanism by which he related to me and how he came to chose me in the first place. This is what he said:

> Now we have talked together, have we not, of the wavelengths which are used in healing. How all psychic development and the use of mediums is dependent upon wavelength and the use that we can make of similar frequencies that lie between the instrument and us. Thus our thoughts are able to penetrate into the mind of the medium. I would like to explain a little the contact that relates us when a medium comes into the orbit of the earth. I will not digress too far to explain why a soul takes upon itself the continuation of mediumship because it often is a continuation. Advanced mediumship is often the result of several incarnations. The mediums that are sufficiently developed to allow strong psychic energy to flow through them in any contained degree have done so previously. So the capacity for mediumship is there within a soul and it is understood that during the process of the developing life the opportunity for mediumship will arise. Thus we hope to expand the growth of both the medium and ourselves. I would like to say expressly that the

co-operation between medium and spirit is a gift to both; a gift from a great source. It is an expression of expansion which lies within the giving of both individuals. This is partnership that is a law and it can only take place in complete acceptance on both sides. We cannot usefully use a vessel that will not mentally accede to the necessary discipline required.

I will try to explain to you how it works and especially in relationship to myself. The psychic body of a medium contains within it the necessary ingredients for the infiltration of the forces of light frequency. This is a gradually expanding ability. The type of psychic energy that is within the mediumistic body refracts light far more quickly than the average. It appears rather as you would imagine a firefly breathing light. This light force within the mediumistic body attracts the corresponding light interchange and a penetration by the spiritual forces that are directed towards it.

When we first come to use our instruments we are aware, not so much of a person, but as it were a vessel of modulating and expanding colour. It is as though, if we could show it to you, you were looking upon a breathing force of light, colour, rather opaque, rather like mists that are changing and interchanging and according to the speed with which this movement goes on so we are able to see the development of the quality in the instrument that we will use. The types of light infiltration attract to themselves the like energy that we project.

We have to wait for the right time for this to happen for we are very dependent upon the physical condition of the medium. The instrument is of course concerned also with human expression. We see, as we look upon our instrument, the best course to pursue. Psychically this is dependent upon the alignment of the instrument in continual frequency. We make use of the psychic centres or chakras, which govern the psychic flow. They must expand and be in alignment. When I speak of alignment in this way I do not mean a straight line, I mean the tuning of one to another as is embodied in a television or radio when the valves are so adjusted that the different parts of the whole are attuned at different ratios to therefore allow a steady flow of alternating electricity to produce the sound and sight waves audible and visible to human ear and eye. So when I speak of the alignment within the instrument, I mean the alignment of the different chakras that have to be used to attain a quality of speed to allow a steady flow. In each body these will be different. You will find, if you look, that the development of the psychic centres in each body is different. Therefore the main objective in tuning is to expand these psychic centres so that they work separately but blend together to allow a steady signal and thus pick up our thought forces. This is a beginning.

From then onwards we gradually tune ourselves into the main light stream, very feeble at first, extracting energy from the medium in gradually strengthening waves. We have to train ourselves also to re-level our own frequency rate so that it is sufficiently comparable with the heavier impetus of the medium. We combine our wavelengths gradually, we could say liquefy the whole, taking from our instrument the necessary ingredients and blending with them. We have to wait for the right instrument before we can talk to you because we are dependent, not only upon the infiltration into the slower instrumentality but we are ourselves dependent and interdependent upon the psychic forces above and therefore quicker than our own which are expanding and flowing through us in the same way. So it is as if there were a telephonic connection between the medium and us and between us and those who use us and who, in their turn, are connected beyond. This is why it is difficult to get completely clear and distinct knowledge for it is not only dependent upon one source and connection, it is dependent on several connections.

Now I will try to speak personally because you have asked me, and explain to you how I attempted to touch and use this way of speaking to you. Please remember I am using an instrument who is not yet trained. I have been aware, since the birth of my medium, that the possibility of the use of this instrumentation might arise during her life span. Also you must understand that within each soul is given the gift of free will so that this service could have been refused. At the infiltration into your world of my instrument, I was aware of a strong point of contact. I can only describe it as an infinitesimal point of understanding and I knew that once again, a line to humanity was open to me. I then drew into myself the re-knowledge of that time of my life in which I was concerned with her. For you must understand that my remembrance of any connection between my instrument and myself had long since passed. Because in the past I have rejected service of this type, I became aware that once more this purpose has been placed before me. This line was a small thread of strength which ran through to my consciousness. It tied and allied itself with the spiritual and psychic growth of the instrument. Although I at no time during these years have infiltrated into the consciousness of the channel, I have been continually aware that at some stage in her development I might be in touch and required to serve.

As time went on the thread became stronger, a light infiltration that would appear to you perhaps like a cobweb, directly connecting us both and strengthening gradually. I then had to learn to enter denser fields of consciousness with my mind. I have not taken upon myself fully a lower astral body. This is why my medium is aware vaguely only of a shape. I use only figuratively the force of my mind to penetrate the dimension that is required of me. I was aware of, in this case, sudden psychic growth of the channel and it was as though a sound ray rang. This is difficult for me to explain because we do not respond to sound as you do, or see as you see. We are aware of colour, light and sound interacting upon each other and interchanging with each other. So I can explain to you only that I was conscious of a warning call or demand, and from that time forward I have attached myself through the group that surrounds my medium. I am now straining her. I leave.

I have often been asked when Nemerah first made himself known to me. I cannot remember precisely but it was around this time. I recall the occasion very well. I was making a bed at home and I heard this rather dictatorial voice, objectively, saying, 'Get a pencil and paper and write this down.' He said: 'My name is Nemerah,' and went on to spell it for me, 'NEMERAH.' I can't quite remember his words exactly but it amounted to the fact that he would be my main control and we would work together for my lifetime, or something to that effect. With that he disappeared and I heard no more for at least six months.

I continued to go to the churches as a speaker and I was asked once or twice to do the clairvoyance and that gradually built up but I myself was very worried by it. I realised it was not, by my standards, anywhere near good enough for public demonstration and also if I had been in the congregation I would have been severely critical. So, of my own volition, I cancelled the bookings I had accepted as a clairvoyant and I wrote to three churches that I knew well, where I had been leading circles and demonstrating psychometry and flower clairsentience. The church that I am most grateful to is Richmond Church. The church owned a house which during the week was used for meetings. I explained that I needed practice, that I did not wish to take any money and that the people who came to my demonstrations should be told that I was learning. They responded to this wonderfully and I had opportunities to give demonstrations, not only of flower clairsentience and psychometry but of trance addresses and demonstrations of clairvoyance. It was a great joy to me when the President, after a demonstration of clairvoyance, said to me: 'Mrs Farrell, you're as good as anybody we get and I would like to pay you.' It is wonderful sometimes to relive the moment of achievement. It was also during these practice sessions that Nemerah took over trance in public.

It was extraordinarily interesting to me because I was aware of the difference in the heightened frequency rate. I was never in deep trance, I could always hear myself. I couldn't make sense of what I was saying but I could hear myself rather as though I was standing behind myself hearing a gramophone record that I couldn't stop. If I listened, or tried to listen, the whole thing would come to an end. I was aware on one of these occasions of losing Nemerah's thread, and it was caught by Saphros. There was no change in actually what was being said but I could feel the difference in the speed ratio. That's the only way I can describe it.

From the time I could hold Nemerah consistently, he has taught me. His methods of teaching vary. They are sometimes visual so that I can see a picture which is instantaneously understandable. For example, I once said to him at the beginning of our association: 'Either it is true or not true, how can both be true?' Instantly a vivid scene flashed in front of me. A man and little boy were standing in front of a garden wall. The man was holding the child's hand. There was a lovely sense of companionship about the picture. They were both contemplating what was immediately in front of them. The little boy completely absorbed in the climbing roses, and the insect life. His father was tall enough to see over the wall. He was equally absorbed in the view beyond. What Nemerah wished to convey was immediately obvious and took far less time than a spoken answer. At other times he has directed me most purposefully towards a book or a lecture that answers my questions, and sometimes by re-reading his lectures with an expanded understanding. When I actually listen to them I understand more than is said. I have deep respect for him. I do not worship him, nor would he wish that I did. He never condemns me, even when I know I have behaved badly. I'm aware of a sense of withdrawal. I feel very uncomfortable. I know, not so much that he is saying I have failed him, as that I have failed myself. He very rarely gives a command without an explanation but if he does I obey it instantly. He has a wonderful sense of humour. He does not compromise or allow me to compromise and has a habit of putting things squarely back on my shoulders.

He has shown truly wonderful compassion and understanding of my human frailty from time to time. Waiting for news of the birth of my first grandchild I felt very alone and distant. My daughter and son-in-law live in South Africa. Quite suddenly the room was full of light. I hadn't asked but I heard Nemerah's voice and I almost saw him. There was a shape of light at one end of the room. 'There is no need to weep, you will hear before the night is out, you have a granddaughter and mother and daughter are well,' and indeed in a few hours my son-in-law contacted me to say this was true.

Examples of his humour are numerous. I was about to give a demonstration of clairvoyance in Canada and was extremely nervous. I was holding myself in so tightly that nothing would have been possible, muttering 'Nemerah are you there, are you there?' Back came this calm voice, 'No' – and of course I went on to the platform laughing. Another time, wishing that I could perhaps find someone who would in some way compare with my husband, I said 'Oh Nemerah, can't you steer someone my way?' He said: 'What? You want to wash shirts again?' Always before a trance lecture, before I let go, I would give Nemerah the format I wished him to use – Mister or Madam Chairman etc. On such an occasion I said 'Nemerah, we are now supposed to say Chair-person' – came the reply 'What? You no longer know if you are men or women? What a pity!'

In January 1971, obviously when Nemerah thought I was ready, he made his wishes very clear. I was booked at Windsor Church as the speaker. The President told me that due to the very bad weather she had for several weeks been let down by the visiting mediums and therefore she herself had had to take the service, and she asked me, for the sake of the congregation, if I would please do the clairvoyance as well. 'I've been doing it now for two or three weeks running. I will help you.' Very loath I did, gratefully aware of her standing behind me ready to come in if I failed. I needn't have worried, my training at Richmond had paid off. The next week I went to another church to be met with the same situation. From then onwards I accepted the full service and for the next four or five years served the Spiritualist churches practically every week, travelling up as far as Huddersfield and down to Bournemouth with a variety all round the country, as do so many. It was excellent training. I've now left the Spiritualist churches because for me at some stage, which comes later on in the story, I did not feel happy or at home there, although I'm deeply appreciative for the opportunities given me.

In 1974 I was asked to do a lecture at the S.A.G.B. I was somewhat surprised but was told once I had accepted, by a friend, that every well-known trance medium had been asked first. Hackles rising I asked Nemerah if I could refuse. As always he said: 'The choice is yours,' however, as I placed my hand on the receiver to ring up and say I'd changed my mind he added: 'Remember there is no room for personal pride in service.' I didn't ring. As a result of that lecture someone wrote to Mr Paul Beard and I was asked to go to the College of Psychic Studies for an interview. I had to give a trance sitting to the President, and a clairvoyant sitting to the then secretary Barbara Somers, well known as a trans-personal psychologist, and to another member of the Council. As a result of this I was asked for a trial period, working first of all one afternoon a week at the College. This was the beginning of my long association with the College.

I realise in retrospect that my training was master-minded completely by Nemerah and looking back I realised that he saw to it that I understood things for myself. Against all odds I was invited to a materialisation demonstration. These days such demonstrations are rare. I was lucky enough to be very near the cabinet, what I saw was unexpected. I was convinced that what I was seeing was genuine. I had imagined ectoplasm as being ethereal, rather like mist, instead of which it was more like rolls of foam which formed upright rods or pillars, the upper part containing a face. It is difficult to describe. Coming round the side of the cabinet towards me I saw the face of my mother appearing through surrounding ectoplasm. Just her face was visible, the rest was shrouded. It was rather like the illustrations of ghosties and ghoulies one sees. I heard her voice, irritably saying: 'Can you see me?' I was somewhat taken aback and just answered 'Yes.' I had no feeling of joy or upliftment and it is not something I would wish to see again. When I think of the effort she must have made I wish I had been able to respond with more warmth.

I had been far more moved by a message I had received from Ivy Northage soon after my mother died. My mother was a passionate animal lover. Next to myself my poodle Sapphy loved and trusted her. We had both been deeply upset when her life span had ended about a year before my mother's. Ivy rang me one day to say that my mother had appeared to her and said, 'Look who I've got.' She went on to say that my mother was 'Nursing your poodle in her arms, on its back like a baby.'

Ivy by then had met my mother many times, knew my family and often seen the dogs. She did not know and had never seen Sapphy held by my mother in this way. My mother, when on her own, always nursed my little dog in this fashion. I was so warmed to think they'd found each other. Ten years later Sapphy still makes her presence known from time to time. As I fall asleep I feel her jump on to my bed.

Another time I had the opportunity of watching a transfiguration medium. He was sitting upright in a chair. He was quite a slight man, narrow faced with greying hair. A black cloth was placed round him and a red light projected on to him under his chin. Suddenly instead of the medium's face there was a rotund bald-headed large Chinese face. Again this kind of phenomena, which I understand was quite prevalent in the past, is rare now. I suppose there are home circles where it still takes place. I was interested as an observer to watch these extraordinary happenings. However, I felt even then, a conviction that they were of the past.

Later in the Spring of 1971, as a result of someone not being able to keep an engagement, I was asked to dedicate Welwyn Garden City Spiritualist Church. I agreed to this not fully understanding what was expected of me. There was a full dedication service in the afternoon. A break for tea, to be followed by an evening of clairvoyance shared with another medium. It was the latter that made me apprehensive. I knew that I had not yet reached a stage in my development where I could maintain my clairvoyance for that amount of time. During the tea break, I found a nearby field and wrapping myself in a blanket, lay on the grass and went to sleep. I awoke with just enough time to change before I took my place on the platform. I did a good demonstration of clairvoyance. I drove home with a singing in my heart. I was ill for about three days afterwards. Thus Nemerah showed me clearly how interchangable psychic and physical energy is. It also taught me how careful I have to be of my own students.

Once I became stronger and able to cope Nemerah made very clear that working conditions had to be accepted. I was expected to do my best in any circumstances. During my first visit to Canada, the heat was excessive. We were driven out to work in a very nice house. There had been no rest period between my afternoon work and the journey. I had about ten minutes to prepare myself for a trance lecture. It was humid and I could hardly breathe. The perspiration was pouring down my face. 'I can't Nem – I simply can't!' 'We will have no histrionics.' I have often thought of that – 'We will have no histrionics' – when I feel temperamental.

Travelling all over the country, for the most part I was very kindly treated. Because of the generosity of a well known medium at that time, Brenda Dunridge, in recommending me, I gained entry to some of the best Spiritualist churches almost at once. I also served others. On one occasion the service was to be held in a school classroom. On asking where I could sit to be quiet and 'tune in' before the service, I was shown into the girls' cloakroom. The only place to sit, a bench opposite the toilets. In answer to my despairing cry of 'I can't' to Nemerah, I heard 'You can.' I did!

I am often aware of his sense of amusement. I was once on a platform in a church and on this occasion was doing the speaking only. It was a small platform, the Chairman, myself and the clairvoyant were on a rostrum together. The Chairman introduced us. 'On my right is Mrs X who will do the clairvoyance and on my left is Mrs Farrell who will give us the address, and I feel like a sausage between two bread rolls.' I was horrified but I could feel Nemerah's amusement.

There was one occasion when his laughter actually shook me. The whole of my solar plexus moved up and down with this tremendous laughter. It was during a sitting at the College. Actually I had great difficulty in sustaining contact with him. The lady who came in started to talk to Nemerah and he did not get a word in edgeways. I often wish I had more sittings like it nowadays! She talked and every now and then she would say 'Don't you agree with me, Nemerah?' Then off she would go again. This went on for the whole of the hour, at the end of which she got up and said 'Well thank you very much, Nemerah, I've had a wonderful sitting' and walked out!

I was shown the variant in the quality of power there is in the earth itself which enables a differentiation in mediumship. I was able to do things in Canada and in America that I haven't been able to do anywhere else. While in Canada, by a most unexpected sequence of events, I went over to Lilydale in America. Lilydale is a Spiritualist village and it comes alive for the whole of the summer and is packed with mediums. They work day and night. It is a beautiful concept. There are Healing Temples and out of door logs where people sit and speak. There is a lake and tall pine trees and the most harmonious surroundings that could be envisaged by anyone trying to portray ideal conditions for mediumship. Unfortunately idealism and reality do not always go hand in hand. I saw much of which I could not approve.

There were demonstrations given at night out of doors. Unexpectedly I was asked to work on such an occasion. I had never given a demonstration in the dark and I wondered how I would do this, always being used to seeing my recipient. The result surprised me. As I got up, very nervous, a brilliant bunch of roses appeared right in front of my eyes and they were outside myself. Now, normally, I never see like this. For this was how it had been at the beginning. I knew the flowers were for a wedding anniversary. I called out 'I have a lady here saying it is my wedding anniversary and I want my husband.' A voice answered out of the darkness. Once I'd got the voice I knew it was the right one, and the evidence followed. I can't remember the details of the rest but the same thing happened each time. An appearance of a bright picture, about a foot in front of my eyes which gave me my first link.

While there, another very extraordinary thing happened. I went with a party from a Canadian church and the President's name was Ruth. I went to bed exhausted about 1.30 a.m. I fell asleep almost immediately to be awakened, very soon afterwards, by the voice of this lady. She had a very distinctive Canadian accent and I heard her say: 'My name is Ruth' and she began to talk about the Spiritualist principles. She spoke very well, very knowledgeably. She seemed to be talking to several other young people who were answering her. I was extremely irritated that she should be talking so loudly just outside my bedroom window. I listened to the whole of this discourse, which went on for, as far as I could judge, about half an hour. I came down the next morning and I noticed that in the lobby of this hotel there were portraits of very famous American mediums who had stayed there. I felt impelled to go towards one and underneath was written *Ruth*. Later, when I saw the President, I said to her 'You were teaching late last night.' 'Well, yes,' she said, 'How did you know?' It transpired that I was able to quote the things she had said. She had had a party of young people and she had been talking to them exactly as I had heard at that time, but she was in a house right the other side of the village. I don't know how to explain that. Whether the two Ruths in any way connected or it was just the extraordinary power, I have no answer, there was no question of being asleep, I was awake.

During the years that I served the Spiritualist churches I

was lucky enough to gain experience as a teacher. I never advertised but at one time I was leading circles at the London Spiritual Mission in Pembridge Place, at Kingston, at Watford and also in a small devoted home circle where I increased my alliance with Nemerah, by taking a class in trance. Thus I learnt to accept the responsibility of teaching. For a long time I always used the method of opening up that I had learned under my training with Ivy Northage.

The small home circle was interesting because in it Nemerah brought through some very interesting teachings and at the same time the circle itself was sitting for direct voice with a trumpet. Now I truly did know that there was not sufficient power in that circle for that trumpet to move. I realised that it was a lovely circle in that its members were very dedicated but physical mediumship needs more than dedication. There has to be the amount of power necessary and there just wasn't. There was, however, one interesting occurrence that I cannot explain. On this occasion I wasn't in trance but taking the circle in a normal way and I realised that the trumpet itself had elongated. It had grown both thinner and longer, stretched to about double its length. The others didn't see it but I did and I've never been able to explain it. This little circle came to an end very suddenly and it was one of the occasions when Nemerah himself had been very firm. We had the usual session and I was told that this was the final meeting. I demurred and suggested I warn them that it would be ending soon. 'No, tonight.' I did as I was asked. They were very hurt and there seemed no logical reason for my doing it but during the next week one of the members had a stroke. Nemerah also explained that the purpose of that particular circle was to train me, and it was time I moved on.

The occasions when I have ignored an express instruction from him are very rare. This happened long afterwards, when I had been teaching at the College for some time. At the end of the term I always ask if there is anybody who does not wish to come back for the next session. I also have the rather sad task sometimes of asking people to leave, when I feel we have not been able to get any further with each other. I can never find a nice way of doing this. People always take it personally. I'm always happier when they say they are going. On this occasion he told me not to include a particular woman. Now I liked her very much. She showed every sign of positive advancement. So I thought I would risk it for just one term. This was a Beginner's Class and I always stress that at no time should they open up psychically and work except in class.

It transpired subsequently that this particular woman was doing this. The result was she had a very bad experience, similar to the kind of experiences that I had had. She was very honest and 'phoned me and with Nemerah's help was able to regain her balance. She came to my home for several weeks running and, under Nemerah's express instructions and exercising, the condition was cured but it taught me a lesson.

Once more out of context but seemingly appropriate here. A long time afterwards, under Nemerah's tuition, I accepted the responsibility of dealing with people who were having the kind of obsessional experience that I had. I was warned by Nemerah to be very aware that he would need to take over at very short notice. This happened again in a beginner's class.

In this class there was a young woman who had been told by a medium that she would die in a car crash before she was forty, and she was then, I think, about thirty-five. Now for any medium to have given such information, by my understanding, showed complete lack of responsibility. However the damage had been done. This very nice young woman was also very worried about difficulties with her husband who disapproved of her taking up development as my husband had once disapproved. In such cases I always leave the decision to them, because it is up to the individual to decide. On this evening this young woman had been particularly worried because on the way to class she had actually seen a car crash. She was obviously in a very bad nervous state. When people are in a state of distress I sometimes suggest that they relax while the rest of the class directs healing towards them. I felt such an exercise would be valuable in this case and decided to use it towards the ending of the class. Normally what happens is that the recipient has a feeling of warmth and comfort and is very much better for the help received. Having remembered my instructions from Nemerah I was particularly careful to be totally aware of him the whole time. To our horror as we sent her healing the young woman began to scream. I rushed to her, took her in my arms and heard myself saying in Nemerah's voice. 'It is alright, it is done, it is over.' It was a terrifying ordeal to undergo, particularly for the people sitting either side of her. For the screams were from someone in agony. She stopped screaming and eventually shaking. When everyone had calmed down she explained that she had in fact experienced the horror of being run down by a car and being pinned beneath it. Nemerah came through again and explained clearly that what had been done now was finished and she herself would not have to undergo such an experience ever and that she would live far beyond forty. For what had been done in the mind would not have to be done again.

Subsequently re-tracing this occurrence, we find here another example of the careful management of a situation. Because that which happened occurred towards the end of class meant that the class that was normally in a room next to ours had left. Therefore the building was practically empty, certainly on the top three floors. So the awful screams were heard by no-one else. I was very worried as to the effects upon the members of the circle, also extremely proud of them. Frightened though they were, not one moved. My first care was for the young woman herself. We had coffee and talked together quietly. I then made sure that she had someone to see her home. When I reached home I phoned all the members of the class. I must admit to feeling quite shaky myself. I found that one or two who lived alone had decided to spend the night together. This was wholly understandable and sensible. They had reacted with amazing courage and maturity.

The following week, when we gathered together again, I asked Mrs Marshall, who by that time was the President of the College, if she would come and talk to them. I had explained the whole situation to her. She related very much to the collective unconscious and between the two of us we explained how the two areas in the patient's mind would come together to achieve such a healing. This is very much Nemerah's work. To the person concerned I had to say that it would be better if she did not come back to class for a while but that I would be available if she wanted help. When she was ready to come back and see us again, she decided of her own volition, that she did not want to continue with general development but wanted to take up healing, and that is what she did.

During the period of my learning, there are many gentle loving memories that stay within my mind. Several of them are concerned with my younger daughter, who at that time was very claivoyant. While I was going through the most difficult time, she was away at Ballet School. She told me later that she knew things were not right and worried about me constantly.

She began to see clairvoyantly an old lady. This lady came often, and when she did, brought with her a serene sense of comfort. My daughter described her as always wearing a particular shawl and brooch. I recognised her from the description as my paternal grandmother, who had died when I was still at school.

When my daughter had gone to boarding school, I had given her my engagement ring. One day she lost it. She searched everywhere but could not find it. To quote her: 'I was so upset. Then I sent up a thought asking to find it. I went straight from the bathroom to my slippers, without even turning on the bedroom light. There it was in the toe. I think it was Grandad who helped (my father). But I don't know why I have that impression.'

The two wave-lengths would be compatible. It seems feasible to me, and a wonderful thought that my family would help my child.

The time came when our loved dog Toby had to be put to sleep. When my husband was alive, as soon as I heard his car returning home I would open the back door and say: 'Go find Daddy' and out Toby would rush. As the vet put him to sleep I had his head in my lap and said: 'Go find Daddy, go find Daddy.' Very upset, I asked that my husband would come and get the dog. I was told that this was not possible, he could not lower his frequency sufficiently but that spirit friends would see that the dog reached him and would tell me. I waited and waited all day, and about 10 o'clock that night someone came and said, 'Your husband has got the dog' and he laughed. He said, 'He is a small man and the dog is so big,' and this was perfectly true. My husband used to nurse this dog on his knee. It was a very large dog and my husband was practically enveloped by it. Still later that night I heard my daughter running up the garden path and tapping on the door to be let in, not even waiting to use her key. I opened the door and she said: 'Mummy, Mummy I've just seen Daddy and he had Toby in his arms.'

I was asked to name a baby at the Christian Spiritualist Church in Tunbridge Wells. The Minister rang me up and asked if I would do this, saying she would send me a written copy of the service so that I could prepare my part in it. It is a charming ceremony. The child is blessed from spirit with the cross and the baptismal names are repeated and an added name given from spirit. The book arrived: while studying I questioned Nemerah, 'Supposing its a tiny baby and I can't tell whether its a boy or girl?' In theory I should have had complete trust at the time! He said very calmly: 'It is a girl and you shall name her Dorothea.' So I accordingly went to the service and blessed the child in the prescribed manner. It was a lovely moment, we seemed surrounded in an extended aura of light and love. As I said 'I name thee Dorothea,' there was a gasp from the mother. Afterwards she told me that it was the name of her very much loved grandmother who had recently died.

When we took our white cat to be put down, she was twenty-one years old; she died with her head in my hand, purring. She had shared so much in our lives. My elder daughter at the age of eight had delivered her. I was out and there was something wrong with the birth. My daughter managed to save two of the kittens. As a young cat, she had been stolen. She had found her way back to us a tattered skinny shadow of herself. Her last years were spent with my younger daughter where she ruled the roost over other younger cats. She has been seen many times and just recently by one of my students in circle who said: 'Mrs Farrell, I see a gentleman whom I think is your husband, he has a white cat in his arms.'

My younger daughter has seen my husband on more than one occasion, but I never have. I am, however, able to hear from him from time to time and I am often conscious of his help. He hasn't changed his personality. I asked him once for personal information about my elder daughter in South Africa, he answered 'If she had wanted you to know she would have told you.' That impressed me very much because that is exactly what he would have said if he had been living here. Also it is very much in accordance with Nemerah's values. Nemerah states that we all have a right to personal privacy. If people come to us and they therefore offer themselves, that is one thing but he always refuses past a certain point to give information about anybody living who isn't in front of me. In the early days of my training I was fascinated by my ability to tune in to particular people. I was able to find out exactly what they were doing at any given time. This was when we happened to be closely allied on the same psychic wavelength. I practised this assiduously proving it to my satisfaction time and time again. One day Nemerah asked me sternly: 'Would you read a private diary?' I understood then the personal implications involved when we accept the responsibility of mediumship. I stopped this at once. I now no longer know if I still have the ability.

Quite when I am not sure, but I began to feel out of tune with Spiritualism as such. At the same time *Man and his Symbols* by Jung fell into my hands. I saw this as a signpost towards a new direction. I was very uncomfortable then at serving the Spiritualist churches because I began to feel that I was being insincere. I was booked through to 1976 solidly and I think it was in 1975 that I was asked by Mr Beard to put all my work into the College. I finished the 1975 bookings but cancelled all those made for 1976, concentrating from then onwards all my work and energy into the College. I agonised a little over it, I still had a desire to be an Estelle Roberts and become well known as a platform medium. It was hard to let that dream go. However, I had a dream.

These dreams are rare but when they come they are unmistakeable. I dreamt that I was on a beach with a lot of people. I was with them and yet observing them. It was a lovely sunny beach, warm, and everyone was very happy. Suddenly the scene changed. The sun was blotted out by dark clouds. There was a terrible storm. The waves became mountainous engulfing the people and they were swept out to sea, screaming, hurt and terrified. Some got washed up on to a little island. I could see them scrambling up on to land. The island seemed sunny; it was covered with trees and was secure. There they lay, panting until they got their strength back and as the waves subsided were able to swim back to shore. On awakening, the meaning of this dream was apparent to me. I saw the College as a place of healing where people can gather strength and find their own way back to meaningful living. That is how it has proved to be. I have seen people come in stressed, demented sometimes, with the agonising conditions of their lives and finding sustenance and help at the College. I see the same people as I pass by, maybe two years later, serene, confident and coping. Perhaps they go somewhere else and we don't see them again but that doesn't matter, they have rested 'on the island'.

As my work with the College gained momentum, and I accepted more and more responsibility, I also had to come to terms with the changing psychological and spiritual aspects of myself. I have already mentioned that I reacted instantaneously to the book *Man and his Symbols*. In the introduction John Freeman speaks of the fact that Jung himself had a dream which was why the book was written, and I quote: 'It was at this moment that he dreamed a dream of the greatest importance to him. (And as you read this book, you will understand just how important that can be.) He dreamed that, instead of sitting in his study and talking to the great doctors and psychiatrists who used to call on him from all over the world, he was standing in a public place and addressing a multitude of people who were listening to him with rapt attention and understanding what he said.' Further along John Freeman mentions the reason for his selection by Jung to collect this work. 'For it very soon came to my knowledge that Jung's reason for selecting me was essentially that he regarded me as being of reasonable but not exceptional intelligence and without the slightest serious knowledge of psychology. Thus I was to Jung the "average reader" of this book: what I could understand would be intelligible to all who would be interested; what I boggled at might possibly be too difficult or obscure for some.'

I would like to make it clear that I have not studied Jungian psychology in any depth at all but on reading this book it made it recognisable for me that I myself was part of a whole, and that any especial aspect of myself such as my mediumistic ability was part of a collective unfoldment and should therefore be recognised at both the spiritual and psychological level. As a very ordinary woman I felt that in terms of related mind and psychism, like John Freeman, what became clear to me would be clear to most. It seemed to me that with this understanding the scientific knowledge of the world itself should be taken into account. Knowledge that was previously part of unconscious expansion is now part of the conscious acceptance of the majority. Children born today, accept very quickly that on touching a button they can see and experience things that are happening at the other end of the world. They don't know why it happens but they accept it. Very soon they come to accept too the atom bomb and the possible devastation that it causes. They come to terms with the laser beam, the hologram and that men walk on the moon. They do not understand, any more than I do, how this is made possible but they know that it is so, and in so doing the mind expansion within the self has an awareness of power and collectivity and expansion that could not be possible even fifty years ago. So that to carry then this knowledge and yet continue to develop mediums in the same way without recognising the mental expansion that has taken place, would be to my mind unprogressive and with little validity.

Of course this didn't happen all at once but gradually, as Nemerah was able to make me understand his meaning. I have made very bad mistakes and I must have fallen into almost every trap that is levelled against mediums. However I have learnt by my mistakes and gradually arrived at the ability to understand that what Nemerah needed of me was my own enlargement. Again I cannot be exact as to when, but he expressed his wish that we should divide our work very clearly into two areas. That of psychic development and what he called 'Deepening Awareness' classes, which were designed to explore the inner realisation of the whole and to find within the self the expansion of the spiritual aspect of the being.

I accepted this and I'll never forget the first class that I gave. I was used by then to the format of psychic development but here I had eight people sitting in front of me expectantly and I had no idea what I was going to do. I had, of course, to link with Nemerah and to listen to him clairaudiently at that time, step by step. The first exercise he gave stays in my mind so clearly. He told me, after a period of meditation, to ask that they stayed with their eyes closed but that they should hold out in front of them their right hand and on it mentally to place that of themselves which they felt was acceptable to the God source. To recognise within themselves that as they, and all of us, are part of the source, that spark of divinity must lie within, for them to accept it wholly, understand it fully and believe in it. To deny it would be to deny the source itself. So therefore each was asked to place mentally upon the hand as a gift that which was acceptable in these terms, that which could be accepted within the self as part of growth, part of love, part of light, any deeds that they felt showed furtherance of understanding. I looked around at the faces and they were imbued with an inner beauty and a joy. 'Now bring your left hand too and place on it that which you find unacceptable both to the source and in yourself.' I couldn't believe it, in no time at all I was looking at eight people with their left hand almost down to the ground and therefore with the imbalance that this caused their right legs were all up in the air, all eight of them! Then Nemerah said, 'Bring the two things together and offer them equally to God for you are seen and loved as you are, not as you would wish to be.' Following from this there were a series of exercises that became part of the teaching.

After a while of course I myself understood them and could give them in my own right, by which I mean that I have understood and am capable of so doing consciously.

Now it was an interesting fact at this point that I had never done any transpersonal psychology but realised that I should, and went to the workshops given by Ian Gordon Brown and Barbara Somers. I was absolutely amazed to find that the exercises that were being given in the awareness classes that I was teaching were very alike, except that in the transpersonal psychology workshops they were written and in mine they were spoken. The overall objectives were similar. I have subsequently done all the workshops with Barbara and Ian and have to thank them for their kindness and generosity in sharing their knowledge with me and in also accepting the areas of difference. The areas of difference are interesting. I would also like to say that whenever I found myself in need of unknotting some tangle within myself I have gone back and done a workshop, and it hasn't mattered then that it had not been in sequence. Although perhaps I found some of it tedious, because I had done it before, there was always some point that let free my particular knot of the moment. That I haven't been able to attend one for some time due to lack of time is my loss. I think it is a very valuable teaching.

After the first workshop an incident pinpointed for me clearly the difference between the two aspects of my work. I left the workshop in the early afternoon to take a service in Essex. It was a long journey and there was very little time between reaching the church and actually taking the service.

When it came to the clairvoyance I realised it wasn't there, it was quite a frightening moment. I explained to the congregation that I couldn't do claivoyance but would do auric reading. They found this perfectly acceptable. Auric reading is really psychometrising a person. If you are a medium you have extra sensory perception in your own right. If you are acutely sensitive, this will be highly attuned and may often pass as clairvoyance. Having been trained by Mrs Northage I very clearly knew the difference. If something is inevitable it is often possible to tell the future at this level and people are interested. It went down very well. I had learned yet another lesson. When working as a sensitive or a medium you withdraw from yourself to let another mind come in. If you are working with the higher intelligence of yourself, you go into yourself to find the enlargement of your own knowledge to give yourself the answers. They are different and this, I have come to the conclusion, is what Nemerah needs – for me to reach the highest point of my own intelligence before I attempt to touch him.

As the years have gone by the two areas of the work have divided considerably, rather as though they had started at the apex of a triangle and spread outwards to a wider and wider base. Within the psychic area the work has changed considerably, my own along with it. According to the structure of my integration with Nemerah's command, so has the exercising and disciplines changed. Once I had accepted that the mind now dominated, he altered our method of opening the psychic centres. He very clearly states that it is no longer necessary, in his opinion, to touch the two lower chakras. Under proper disciplined direction there is no danger in this but these two chakras are very allied with the sexual energies, very basically related to the earth and within the concept of mind energy they are no longer part of positive attunement. Then gradually he has come to teach us that once having lost the physical body the intake of energy differs and that therefore the equivalent of our breathing is of a different nature, lighter and faster in intake of energy. So that while we are open there is a definite breathing rhythm that is quicker than ours and relates mentally to the body that we next inhabit. Obviously this cannot be in entirety since we are recognisably encased in a slower energy but mentally we try to relate to the differentiation in breathing and we begin with recognising the psychic energy at the heart centre. This has come gradually as I have been able to understand and adapt to it. Also we start by integrating at the spiritual level. Though the leader of a circle, I cannot command the inner core or note of any individual's attunement with the height of their own aspiration. That is absolute unto themselves, their note, their own harmonic. We start by feeling the heart fellowship of the circle and the warmth that it brings, then each finds their own spiritual height, their own spiritual note. Only when this has been brought down individually do we relate to the specialised breathing which is our part of opening the psychic centres to the intake of increased energy.

The awareness area of the work has broadened considerably over the years. From that small beginning of the first awareness class, there has grown a widening expansion in understanding human need. Because of my experience of obsession in the beginning I am able to understand fully the loneliness of people in despair. At one time we did start sessions at the college whereby I saw people who were undergoing this type of stress, for three-quarters of an hour once a week for four weeks running. This had to be discontinued as I soon realised that it was not nearly long enough. If I undertake such work nowadays, I see people at home but carry the interviews on for much longer than four weeks.

Aware of my psychological, psychic and spiritual make-up, Nemerah has been able to use this extended knowledge of spiritual law to teach a great deal about the understanding and conquering of fear. There has been quite a lot of work done on these lines, both with individuals and to an extent publicly.

Nemerah teaches that fear has its element of value in the world in which we live. We are conditioned to it from a very early age. We learn to protect ourselves as a result. If the fear is conscious and understandable, we learn to adapt and accept the emotion without too much hurt. It is the underlying and unexplained fears that cause the lasting damage.

These often begin in childhood and are suppressed. He says that sometimes it may be better to allow a child to hurt itself slightly physically, than to cause far more harm psychologically by being over protective, resulting in the child becoming unduly fearful.

As always, he advocates balance in all things. If fear is our master then we are emotionally crippled. In such cases it is important that we find and face our fears or else find means to negate them. He speaks of the dark area of ourselves that we are fearful of uncovering; once laughingly commenting that we are all afraid of being found out!

This in turn causes us to adopt and project false personalities upon which we build at our peril. For sooner or later cracks will appear, and confusion result. It is better to know ourselves as we are than to think we are better than we are. That way we can at least build on sure foundations.

His teaching is controversial, in that he says that in many cases it is unnecessary to undergo long analysis nor is it necessary to find the origin of the fear. Of course he does not mean in every case. He says that to find a way of curing the fear and be without it is enough.

Some unexplained deep seated fears are the result of collective experiences from past incarnations. To explore their origins can, he says, in some cases be helpful. Not always so. I remember a case of a person made miserable by claustrophobia. Ten years of analysis had not altered it. Nemerah told me that it came from a dreadful experience in a past incarnation of being walled up alive. 'Do not recount it, it will not help.' Instead he offered certain suggestions and disciplines. I had a letter some while later saying, though not by any means cured, the condition was much improved, and was to a degree manageable.

I have a fear of heights. I do not feel it would help me over much to be told, as a friend of mine was, that my fear came from being thrown over a cliff as a human sacrifice. I have to admit this is a fear I haven't faced. If necessary I force myself to overcome it. If it is unnecessary I give way to it. On the whole it does not spoil my life.

Once we have understood and conquered a fear, we have grown in understanding. So in one aspect, fear itself has become friend and teacher. If we are able to face and alleviate one major fear we will often find that unnamed subterraneous lesser fears have also disappeared. I can only accept that in my own case it was so, as I have mentioned earlier in the narrative. It has also proved to be the case with others who have sought Nemerah's help.

Logical fear is understandable, illogical fear is much more difficult to deal with. In my own case Nemerah made this very clear to me, also clarifying for me the issue of 'a fear faced is a fear halved'. It was Christmas time, about 4 o'clock in the afternoon. I was in the middle of frantic preparations for the evening Christmas night dinner and the festivities to follow – the tree and the presents and all the rest of it. The family were coming to me and my daughter had been ill and it was hoped that she would be well enough to come. My son-in-law 'phoned to say that she was considerably worse, her temperature very high and there would be no question of him being able to leave her, let alone her coming. I went on, disappointed but realising there were others coming as well for whom I was responsible. I suppose it must have been about half past five, when actually laying the table, that I began to shake all over with an over-mastering fear.

I became absolutely convinced that my daughter was going to die. I was so petrified that I couldn't even think. I mentally screamed for Nemerah. He could have alleviated my fear completely as he has done on many occasions since, by saying 'Your child will not die,' but instead I felt his strength and his calmness overshadowing me. He did not tell me either way. He said 'Face your fear and reach the conclusion.' Step by step I went through the possibility of losing my daughter, and the agony it would entail, until I reached the point whereby I had to face unconditionally the fact that should she die she would be alright. Her father and others who loved her dearly would be there to meet and look after her. Mine would be the loss; in some strange way *that* I could accept. My fear didn't go, nor indeed my pain. Even in retrospect thinking about this now, I know, should it happen my agony would be intense, but knowing that she would be alright and looking at it clearly somehow altered the concept of the terror. Instead of it mastering me I could face it. I didn't lose the terror but I lost the terrorising effect of total immobility. I was able to complete the evening. Within a day I knew she would be alright. I then recognised the illogicality of my fear based on the emotional area of myself when relating to my family.

It would seem a harsh way of dealing with such a situation. I know I thought so at the time. I can only say that there have been innumerable occasions when Nemerah has dealt with my human weaknesses and fallibility with indescribable compassion, gentleness and understanding.

One day, again I'm not quite sure when, Nemerah made it clear to me that the trance condition would go. He explained that we had reached a stage in our communication where he could expand my mind no longer in the trance condition. My trance had never been a deep one. I was always aware of the voice going on, rather like standing behind a record, and always aware that at any time I could step back and stop it. I'm not quite sure but I think I understood that the only way he could develop me further was if I was prepared to go into a complete oblivion and become totally unaware of anything that was taking place. I had only ever had one experience of this, and that unbeknown to myself. I had been giving an interview to someone who had asked for trance. I was very very tired and fell asleep. I awoke to the fact that the bell in my room had rung, indicating the end of the session. With a feeling of guilt I realised, or thought I did, that I would have to take my client back to the desk and say the interview had been a failure as I have to do when these occasions arise, but also to admit that I had been asleep! In acute embarrassment I got up to do just that, when she said: 'Oh Mrs Farrell, thank you so much, that was a wonderful sitting.'

Call it failure in me, I only know that I could not voluntarily allow that total oblivion. I accept that I may have failed Nemerah but I also accept that he knew his medium. He did not offer nor ask me to make the choice. He knew what my answer would be. When he told me this I had a moment of panic, wondering how I would face the hour long lectures which were always totally unprepared. I said to Nemerah, 'If I asked you could I trance?' He answered, 'Of course, I would not put my medium in a position of embarrassment.' A moment or two of silence and then: 'But I hope you would not put me in such a position either.' From that time onwards the trance condition has stopped, except on one or two occasions when I have been particularly tired and Nemerah has chosen so to work for my sake. Also on one other occasion, when I had explained before I accepted an engagement that I no longer tranced, only to find that I had been advertised as a trance medium. On this occasion I told

Nemerah what had happened and said I would accept his decision and on that occasion we used trance.

We now work inspirationally and by that I mean that I myself reach the highest point I can before we begin. I'm aware of deepening my attunement to the highest frequency point I am capable of reaching and then touching the mind energy that I relate to, which I recognise as Nemerah's. It is difficult to explain the difference that has come about through the years in which I have worked this way. In a way I had a feeling of loss first of all because I have become less and less conscious of Nemerah's personality. It is so much now a connection of mind; his mind, his thought instantaneously expressed through my mouth with my personality. That is the nearest I can come to describe it. I am completely conscious of what I am saying but I cannot relate it in meaning to the sentence before. If I try to do this consciously I would stop it exactly as I would have done when in trance. I'm always highly sensitive and very nervous before taking the platform for a lecture and I like to have at least half an hour by myself beforehand to attune to Nemerah. I often structure within my mind how I think the lecture will go, only to find as I open my mouth, that we are going in a completely different direction.

Once having started I am no longer nervous, I know the connection is there and I'm alright. I then have total concentration in what I am doing, and there is no room for nervousness. The questions after the lectures I find I usually enjoy. I like the reaction of the audience and at that point it is almost as though Nemerah himself withdraws even further, leaving me to deal with the question period. I have assimilated his teachings to such a degree that I know what his answers will be, therefore it is unnecessary for him to stay so closely allied. However, if I am nonplussed he is back within an instant.

I remember one such occasion when someone asked why

it was that most women have male guides and male mediums have male guides also. Nemerah's answer was quite interesting. He says that the usual thing would be the opposite as in a case of the animus to the anima in Jungian psychology, but that in mediumship everyone, male or female, is in fact using the female intuitive aspect of themselves.

While lecturing sometimes, if appropriate, Nemerah will feed into my mind a particular episode of something that happened to me. On such an occasion he will withdraw completely, I can feel this, and I tell that part totally from my own memory; as he has explained, the occurrence happened to me. I went through it, he did not. The attunement between us has heightened rather than lessened over the years we have been working like this. Particularly within the last two. I'm no longer aware of a feeling of loss, in fact it is almost one of gain. I know that his wisdom and knowledge are far beyond my own but that he is ready to share it to whatever degree I can expand my vision and mental capacity to attune to it. In a personal sense I am still aware when I fall below his standards and have the same sense of withdrawal as I always did, the withdrawal without condemnation. It poses the question of course as to whether in Jungian terms Nemerah is indeed my animus. I can only say with all honesty that I do not believe so. I have a higher self of course, as does everybody, and it is this self that I must seek before I attune with Nemerah, but I believe that I relate to a different personality and a different mind.

I have come to the conclusion that I must be one of many who mediumistically are bridging a gap between the old forms of mediumship and what must become the new. I believe that we have to find a way of reaching communication that takes into account, and accepts, the enlarged consciousness. I believe that the trance condition itself is part of the past, that the new forms of communication in those terms will be very much of mental capacity. It is less onerous on the medium's physical body for a start. I believe that physical mediumship as demonstrated in materialisation, wonderful though it was for those who were able to do it beautifully, is also of the past and that the corresponding mediumship will show itself in the future in some form of picture above the medium's head, perhaps rather like a hologram. These things will be found, I'm quite sure, not perhaps in my time but in the future. I also believe that eventually the force-fields of energy, electrical impulses, will become so great that those accepting intensified forms of mediumship, such as perhaps producing picturisation, will have to withdraw into seclusion and will become a form of enclosed order, rather like a priesthood.

Has Nemerah told me these things? No, not as he sometimes imparts information. They have come in visionary flashes, usually when I'm out walking. I am very dependent upon earth attunement. I get my strength back from walks by the water and amongst trees and beautiful places of nature, and it is then that these things come into my mind. They seem a far cry from the small circles that I teach and I realise that few, if any, will attain these objectives; but my students will go beyond me and others beyond them, and in the acceptance of the possibility so eventually will be the link that attains it. Someone has to begin and without vision there can be no attainment.

As my teaching has altered, as I have come to understand more, imperceptibly I have realised that my capacity as a medium in terms of relating in private interviews, has altered also. Originally I felt that my job was to prove survival, to the best of my ability, and that was it; until one day Nemerah gently suggested that we were there to help people in whatever capacity was best for them. Therefore at times it could be helpful to them to advise them upon their material needs, perhaps to give them assurance of the future, as well as to put them in touch with those that they had lost. In the first days, when I worked at the College, if a trance sitting was requested with Nemerah he did not, I think, relate them to people in spirit. I did that consciously clairvoyantly. Once the trance condition had gone I tried to divide the interview roughly into three parts, the spiritual teaching from Nemerah, relating sitters to friends they have lost, and help with personal conditioning of their lives.

Over the years that I have been working, the range of communication that I have been instrumental in achieving has altered considerably. In 1977 I kept for one year a journal. I used to write it every night on my return from the College and there I listed the type of sittings that I had had and any particular item that interested me. I don't believe that I could do this now because my memory of the interviews that I give is erased so very quickly. I can only remember parts of certain communications if they have interested me personally because of the type of communication. In 1977 I wrote consistently and therefore have a record of some of the more interesting types of communications that I have been privileged to take part in.

Some communications that perhaps give me much pleasure in remembering were a series from the writer Monica Baldwin. It is also another example of threads being drawn together. For many years previously, I had read her book *I Leap Over the Wall*. It was an account of her agonising decision to leave the closed community of nuns in which she had been since she was sixteen and a half, and to come out into the world. After reading the book I was very much moved by this and I remember thinking to myself, 'I would love to meet this woman.' And so perhaps in a way I have done so. My sitter was a very kind woman and I know that she will not mind me telling this story. I remember it very clearly. She came into my room and gave me a watch. I very rarely hold anything but this time I accepted it. It was a man's watch and as I handled it, I knew it was habitually worn by a woman. I said so, giving it back to her. She admitted I was right. From then onwards the evidence poured through, I could hear her so clearly. I eventually said, 'This has to be Monica Baldwin' and it was so. From then onwards this sitter came to see me many times. She was writing the biography of Monica Baldwin. I don't know whether she has ever completed it. Each time she came Monica Baldwin produced new evidence. One of the many facts given, which were both human and completely evidential, came when my sitter had complained of being cold in the particular hotel in which she lived. Monica Baldwin said: 'You have still got my dressing-gown' and my sitter laughed and agreed that this was perfectly true, although she had forgotten about it. Apparently she herself had given this particular dressing-gown to Monica Baldwin. It was a beautiful, warm garment and she had left it packed away with other things in the country and it would be very useful now. Another item of interest she gave was the fact that she was a great collector of newspaper cuttings. Monica used to cut out articles that interested her, and she went on to say that my sitter had got all that evidence. She named a particular suitcase or box where these articles could be found. Again my sitter subsequently told me these things proved to be correct. I was able to hear Monica Baldwin with absolute clarity and her evidence was incontestable time after time after time.

One day my sitter arrived carrying a book saying she had felt she was the gift bearer for she had been asked the night before, directly from Monica Baldwin, to bring me this book and to inscribe it as from herself. It is a copy of *The Called and the Chosen* and inside is written:

> To Elizabeth Farrell – I can never thank you enough for all that you have made possible and for the joy which it has

brought. This book is only a token but it brings all my gratitude and appreciation. Monica Baldwin.

I very much value this gift, sent to me from someone living behind the curtain we call death.

At this time the effects upon me of the different types of communication were very varied. At one interview I was aware that my communicator in some way was still very much attached to the earth, for I 'became' him. I realised that I was rather a tall man, with what appeared to be half of the right side of my face blown away. Then I knew that it had not been blown away but had been eaten away gradually right through to the bone by a terrible cancer. I could no longer speak and it was an agonising condition. I described this to my sitter, who was his wife, who accepted that this was indeed the condition at his passing. I also had been walking with a stick, and was very thin and emaciated. As I gave her the condition, it was wiped from me and I realised that now I was walking upright, very much more filled out, that my face was whole and I found myself patting my face and saying to her directly: 'Look what they've done to my face, look what they've done to my face, they've mended it, wonderful what these chaps can do now.' And I could see as he saw, and I was in what he thought was a hospital still on earth. Since then I have seen it many times or, similar ones. There seemed to be a central courtyard with a fountain in the middle. I find it difficult to describe because although the effect was of water flowing in the fountain it was really of light, and in retrospect now, as I am describing it, it seemed to fall on flowers. Leading off the courtyard were corridors. The one I could see was lighted. Looking down it longitudinally there was free passage way on one side. The other was divided into cubicles by partitions of glass-like substance on three sides. In some of the cubicles I could see figures lying on a kind of couch, also glass-like but opaque. There were no bedclothes or pillows, though some did have support under the neck. All were resting peacefully and comfortably. Here and there white coated figures moved quietly, as one would expect to see doctors or nurses in a hospital. As I am writing I am seeing it again in my mind. I'm not quite sure now whether I'm relating to that one occasion or other similar scenes in which I have been concerned since. Examples of this kind have always been very consistent both in what I have seen or heard.

The man continued excited, 'Look, isn't it wonderful, the walls are of glass but I can walk through them into the garden beyond.' There were beautiful gardens and scenes beyond and these people could literally walk through walls if they so wished. He then asked his wife if, when she came again she could bring his dressing gown. This surprised us both. After that the parents communicated. In my journal I haven't written whether his or hers, but parents came. They explained that they had met him. They gave evidence to the wife of their identity too, enough for her to recognise them. They told her, because of the very depleted and difficult passing and the years of pain that he had suffered prior to this, it was taking time for him to be nursed back into the acceptance of the fact that he had died and that he was whole. It must be done gradually. They told her that when she slept she left her body and with other members of the family visited him. He thought that these visits from his family still on earth were the reality and the contact with his dead parents was a dream. Since then I have participated in many communications where similar evidence has been given. This was the first time that I had actually experienced any physical impact on my own body of the change before and after death.

Another time my sitter was an elderly lady. She accepted much of the evidence that I gave her but seemed dissatisfied in some way. She told me that the communicator had always called her by a particular pet name and asked if I could get it for her. I always freeze if somebody asks me something particular. I know this is a failing within myself but I'm always so nervous that I will not be able to get it, that indeed I can't. I became so tense that it puts paid to any hope of complying. I asked with all my heart for help. There appeared in front of my eyes the drawing of a dove. A line was drawn through the head and above it was written the letter B. Stupidly I said 'Bird.' 'No,' she answered, 'it was Bove.' If only I had been quick enough! In a way this is an excellent example of something I now explain to my students. When we cannot hear, as I had cut off my hearing then, if the evidence is being given, the mind, through the subconscious will supply the nearest equivalent that it can. It is valid communication as far as it goes but it is open to misinterpretation. Its a kind of visual shorthand if you like and can be useful. It is no substitute for the reality of true clairaudience and clairvoyance. I would add however that sometimes any kind of communication is better than none.

Another time, towards the end of the sitting, my sitter asked if I could give a specialised aspect of his communicator's life. As I froze my right hand came up and hit my right ear very hard. I said 'He was deaf in his right ear.' 'Goodness gracious me,' he replied, 'So he was, I had forgotten.' As we were speaking together, flashing into my mind came a picture of the House of Lords. I mentioned this. He was delighted, saying that was what he had wanted. His friend had been a Lord.

I am constantly surprised by the trivia of some evidence that elicits instant conviction. Comparatively recently my communicator was Arthur Koestler. I was aware that my client was not happy with the evidence I was giving. I was very worried by this. For I felt I could hear quite clearly what Koestler was saying. My client could not accept that he would say such things. There are times when I cannot provide a proper link. There are many reasons for this. If this happens when working at the College, I explain to my clients that we are not on the right wavelength. I then take them back to the reception desk and their fee is returned to them. I dislike doing this intensely, always feeling it is my failure. This time I was seeing my client in my own home. I truly felt that what I was giving I was receiving from Arthur Koestler. This caused a certain difficulty between us. Then I heard Koestler say rather irritably, 'Tell him I had all my own teeth.' It seemed an inconsequential, almost flippant remark to make as opposed to the rest of the communication. It was accepted absolutely and with general laughter, the situation thus dissolving pleasantly.

The longer I have done this work, and in some ways the more adept I have become in relating to communication, the more I realise how very little we know. Nowadays my interviews and the way they evolve follow no particular pattern. The method of communication seems to vary almost from interview to interview. I have no simple answers. Something I have always found difficult to understand, and still do, is my inability to recognise particularly well known personalities. For instance I remember an interview when my communicator was Joyce Grenfell. She came through I think in a relationship with a sister-in-law. I gave a certain amount of evidence about her saying, 'This is your sister-in-law,' I remember my sitter saying, yes, that I was quite right and then added 'Surely you recognise her, this is Joyce Grenfell.'

Another time Aldous Huxley communicated. I had read his books and also much about him. During the interview I had no awareness that it was Aldous Huxley communicating until at the very end when I said to my client, 'I was to say to you, "Brave New World".' Then of course I realised it must be Aldous Huxley. That was one of my memorable sittings. I remember these types of interview because they are comparatively rare. I do not remember much of what is actually said. They register because of the impact on me. They are the type of sittings where I am surrounded in light. The ceiling of the building goes. I myself am aware of immensity, and unclouded vision. I've come to the conclusion that when this happens it is because there is an enlargement in the spiritual sense in both the communicator and the sitter, a mental expansive capacity and love between them. The love in a far greater sense perhaps than the personal issues involved.

One day someone came to see me to try to get in touch with either their mother or mother-in-law. I'm not quite sure which. I cannot recollect either if I was able to get any contact at all. Certainly I had no knowledge that the communicator was a great friend of mine. Her name was Joan Clayton. She was of supreme integrity both as a person and as a medium. She had helped me a great deal. She had acted as my Chairman when I gave trance classes over some years. She also helped me with workshops. I liked her very much and I could never understand why I was not able to recognise her.

Another vivid memory I have is of communcation received from the well known colour healer Ronald Beasley. The man who came to see me was a great friend of his. As he came in I noticed he was wearing a large insignia of some sort on a ribbon round his neck. It could have been a cross. Almost immediatcly I felt my fingers elongate to three or four times their normal length. I could see my hand elongate and colours pouring from all of the fingers. It was quite lovely. As I was giving the interview I remember saying to the client, from my communicator, that the ornament he was wearing had been a gift from him. This was so. He went on to say that he was killed in a bus while travelling in India. It was then I realised who it must be. It is the only time I have sensed such an out-pouring of absolute colour through the hands in this way. The examples that remain so vividly within the mind can be relived. As I tell of them I relive them now. There is a validity in the interchange that retains vitality. Just as sometimes the opposite applies.

I myself understand fully that once we have truly communicated with those we love, they themselves feel a sense of release. They want to reassure us they still live, especially when they are aware of grief. As I play my part as the connecting link I sense their relief at being able to assure their loved ones of their continued existence. Having made contact perhaps several times, having said in effect, I am here, I am alive, I love you, try not to grieve for me, their sense of a job done is almost tangible. Sometimes I am irritated personally by the fact that people have many interviews with different mediums time after time, after time. In such cases I feel the true essence of communication has gone. What remains is a kind of replay, rather as though they've left a recording behind which can be retouched by me. What I feel is totally different, its a kind of deadness. I feel I want to say in such cases: 'Look, they have proved again and again that they exist, they love you, let them be.' These are the occasions when I am partly in agreement when people say leave them alone. We cannot bring anyone back who does not want to come though sometimes perhaps we ask too much. There is a sense of balance within all this. If sometimes the need arises for a 'long distance telephone call' then by all means make it, do not make it habitual, or the centre of your life.

When I tranced, as I have already mentioned the spiritual and personal advice was given by Nemerah, the clairvoyance by me. Now, as we have altered the way in which we work together this situation does not arise. I also feel that my sensitivity towards communication has altered too. The change has been gradual. The communications I receive now are less tangible, in some way inconclusive, though they seem to have other attributes.

Many who come to me do not want communication. If they do it is very much more the touching of two people sustaining a relationship through space and time, accepting growth potential where each exists. This does not prove survival in the accepted sense, only inasmuch that the personalities do not alter. People will say to me: 'That is exactly what he would have said.' Or perhaps exclaim: 'Oh that's her, that's her.' The evidence they are receiving could not be offered as proof, inasmuch that the communicators talk about the lives they are now living. My clients will often respond with understanding, saying such things as 'I can imagine that would interest him' – or 'He always wanted to know more on that subject' – 'She was always saying if she had her time over again she would do so and so.' They are recognised by mannerisms, terminology, phraseology, or movement of hands and body. More importantly, sometimes my sitters will themselves be able to sense the presence of the person they love. On the other hand I do not now seem to receive the kind of factual evidence that I have been able to in the past.

Fairly early on, while working at the College, I found that it was far better not to accept a double sitting. Whether they were parents who had lost a child, or a daughter and mother who had lost father and husband, I realised that it was better to see both separately, partly because the relationship is so different between one person and another. I would find my wavelengths intercepted in a strange way and very often became fused. Also it was difficult to be totally open because, for instance, the relationship between a husband and wife has aspects which do not concern their children. A discarnate father would say something about his wife perhaps to a daughter that he would not say with his wife present for fear it would hurt her. So I always now see people individually other than if there is some special reason, such as a language problem.

I have also learnt over the years not to let myself get personally involved or judgemental when giving a sitting. Sometimes it is difficult. It doesn't happen very often, but occasionally I have had a three way communication. The communicator himself talks to me and asks me to say something slightly different. I am reminded of one case I have written up in full in the journal I kept in 1977. Its a very good example of what I mean. My sitter was a woman who had been pointed out to me as having lost her son in an accident. So when I recognised her when she came into my room I told her what I knew but that I would do my best to try to contact her son. He communicated very quickly. I was very pleased at some of the evidence. He gave his age, characteristically referred to his home as 'the dump' (I almost didn't give this!) said that he used to dance his mother round the kitchen, and that there was 'A black mark stacked against me at the University.' She agreed all this was true. Then he continued, 'There is an area of forgiveness necessary between us now. We always argued a lot but I adore her.' She accepted this also. It then transpired that he had made a will and his mother was having it set aside. She told him she was sorry but she felt he had been very unfair not to have considered his brothers or indeed her; leaving a large insurance policy which would go to, or should have done, to someone else. I mentally asked him if he minded this. He replied, 'Yes I do, but don't put it like that to my mother, it will upset her.' The fact remained that his mother who loved him so much was trying to stop his will going through, nor would she listen to any comment I made about this. What interested me was that here was an argument between them continuing over the grave so to speak, with me able to speak independently to him in my mind, and in words to his mother, with him leaving me to find a way of conveying the fact that he resented what she was doing without upsetting her! I incidentally felt highly irritated with her. On the one hand she told me how she adored him, that he was advanced spiritually and had told her he would die before he was twenty-two. Then she set aside his wishes. I really couldn't equate with this, I felt myself mentally siding with the communicator and I realised afterwards that this is not my function and I should try to remain totally uninvolved.

For over two years, 1976 and 1977, I worked every week with the help of Mrs Billie Hamilton, an Inner Brother of the White Eagle Lodge, in trying to reach Nemerah more truly. This was teaching for myself and I sat with Mrs Hamilton for an hour each week and what came through she transcribed. She is yet another to whom I owe a debt of gratitude. I have kept some of these transcripts and refer to them from time to time. I realise how much Nemerah is concerned with the relationships of people and he talks always of the importance of our growth in these relationships. For instance I quote here . . .

> Gradually you gain increased vision and understanding when you relate in trust and fulfilment to another through earthly relationships. Between husband and wife, through the true concept of friendship that exists between that of mother and child, father and son, brother and sister, sister to sister. The essential factor is the true giving of oneself to another at whatever level the relationship demands. Unifying love is the part of comprehension and each individual must find his own way through a complexity of co-ordinations and inter-relating relationships, all demanding different aspects of experience. The governing factor to be one whereby you give and receive according to the capacity of the relationship to further itself in terms of mutual expression. Where there is no trust there is no reality, where there is no gift there is no truth, where there is no demand there is no growth. Co-ordinate within yourself the level of your capacity to give, unify the reality of

yourself and make of yourself a true vessel to receive of the divine guidance that is yours.

In making a record such as this, obviously the examples of communication chosen are the most interesting. When one relates to people as I do, month after month, year after year, the average sittings would be average. One end of the spectrum being those that I have already referred to in which I am not able to do anything for my sitter at all and the other end of the spectrum being the contrasting, occasionally more spectacular interviews. In between come a variety of average sittings. My relationships with my clients have been on the whole very good. They've been very kind to me and I have received many many letters of generosity and appreciation after having had an interview. I myself am very grateful for those I receive. In all these years I have received exactly seven unpleasant letters. Three came together in one week in 1987 which really did throw me! I keep none, the reason being that the first unpleasant letter I ever received some while ago was extremely virulent. I felt undeservedly so in the violence of its attack. People have every right to complain if they feel I have not done my job. But I was upset by this letter and burned it, following a cleansing process that Nemerah teaches. I realised then that if I kept only the ones that were pleasant and which were complimentary I was, if you like, loading the evidence in my favour. I also understood that many people are kind by nature and perhaps have been dissatisfied and not written. Also I don't like accumulated paper. When people write to me I am touched, gratified and I keep and re-read the letters perhaps for several weeks so that the kindness seeps into me. I am warmed. Sitters are very generous in writing to me after they have refuted evidence. I'm thinking of a particular case of a lady who wrote to me two years after seeing me. Apparently I had said in the interview that her grandfather had nursed her on his knee and that she had been one of three children. She had told me that her grandfather had died before she was born and that she was one of two. Subsequently the items given had proved to be right and she wrote to tell me so. There have been many letters of this nature. Unfortunately I have very likely, in fact nearly always, forgotten the entire episode which doesn't mean that I am less grateful for receiving these letters. I have come to terms with the fact too that at each interview I give I truly do my best and as such, good or bad, that is all I am able to do. Sometimes I have persisted with a sitting at the request of my client against my better judgement and almost always in those cases the results have been inconclusive. After I have suggested I would like to terminate the interview they have pleaded with me to continue and I have continued, the resulting sitting has proved to be ineffective and unsatisfactory. I know I should abide by my first impression. The problem is that we who are doing this work know that we are there to help people and that is our main concern. It is hard to disappoint people.

PART FOUR

THE UNFOLDING JOURNEY

WHEN ACCEPTING STUDENTS for training I ask that they read four books. *The Chakras* by Leadbeater; *Forty years a medium* by Estelle Roberts; *Many Mansions* by Gina Carminara; *Memories, Dreams and Reflections* by Carl Jung. For me the variety of these books gives the area of the expansion within the self that is required for general mediumship. An understanding of the psychic mechanism, in the variety of all types of mediumship as shown by the life of Estelle Roberts. The concept of reincarnation, beautifully told and explained in *Many Mansions* by one of the greatest psychics of this age, Edgar Cayce. Finally in the expanded consciousness as understood and explained by Jung. All these areas I feel are important in undertaking development of oneself in relation to the mediumistic quality.

Nemerah himself does not advocate research into past incarnations on the part of individuals. He is very adamant that we are concerned with this life. It is in this life that we weave new material into the pattern of our tapestry. He maintains that in trying to find out too much about our past incarnations we are very dependent upon interpretation given to us and this may be good or bad according to the ability of the interpreter. Very much better, he says, to concentrate on the life that we have today. He himself sometimes gives small pieces of information about past incarnations if he thinks they are relevant and would be helpful in such a case. I therefore have never sought to research into my own in this way. I feel that if it is necessary I would be shown it when I have perhaps reached a stage in my spiritual development where such knowledge would have overall value.

It is difficult to itemise any one aspect of Nemerah's teaching. Paramount is his insistence that we come to terms gradually with the understanding of our involvement as part of a whole; that we are part of nature, part of the natural laws, part of each other, part of God's consciousness and therefore cannot be separated from God. That the individual pathway to expansion comes through a variety of experiences and each one has its own validity according to the need of the moment. He teaches that above all our relationship with each other is the most important of all learning experience. That we ourselves, as part of God consciousness, have within us the reality of our own purpose to experience the now, to give in principle to the whole of life, to acknowledge our place in it at the moment and to portray within the example of our lives that which we believe. The true essence of expansion, he says, is in the understanding of our place in time as related to the people that we have chosen to be with. To use wisely the potential of the life that we live. At no time can we be separated from the God consciousness for we are part of it. In so accepting this responsibility, our own generative process becomes important with every act, every word, every expanded thought. In such realisation we ourselves have to accept above all personal responsibility. The love that we have within ourselves to offer to each other through our hands and our hearts and our deeds. I quote here an extract. Nemerah is talking about love between people:

Love is what we are, what we say, what we do. It is in

the kindness and gentleness one to another in the touching of spirit that love grows.

Then hold your love lightly while you have it, do not crush it. Whether it be between parent and child, husband and wife or friend and friend. For love is laughing, lyrical and lovely. It is generous, gay and carefree. It is as waving corn and summer breeze. It is in the 'seeing' in the living of all growing things the touch of the hand of God.

Love is all of strength
The might of certainty
The coolness of clear sight
Quietude of knowledge
In darkness and in light

More difficult for me to grasp was, once more, his insistence on balance when he teaches about love, as we are involved in our own understanding of the word. I enjoy giving presents, especially pretty things. I get tremendous pleasure out of Christmas and the excuse to indulge my own extravagance, especially towards those I love or have admiration for. I did this with friends to excess sometimes. I can honestly say that I never did so with the intention of like return. It was only born upon me gradually that is is easy to be generous when you love people. I did not have equal generosity when it came to impersonal giving! I did not have sensibility enough to understand that we can cause embarrassment by a surfeit of our emotional need to express our love. Not only in gift giving but in our demand of their time, in our desire to be always included in their entertaining, being resentful of their ability to enjoy without us. We cannot love too much. In our loving we must learn balance in giving what the other needs. I quote again:

Try not to ask of another more than he can give. Do not give to another more than he is able at that time to receive.

In our need to grow we ourselves have to accept tools of experience and as such often become members of a particular type of teaching. All have validity according to our need of the moment. Above all he advocates that we ourselves have no right to condemn at any point. There is, and he stresses this again and again, a great difference between condemnation, and the inner realisation that we have come to a place in our own personal growth towards spiritual expansion, where we can no longer accept certain acts or certain ways of life, or certain teachings. These things which we can no longer condone, we have not the right to condemn, for that which we find most abhorrent has at some time been part of ourselves. This means in effect that we are faced constantly by choices for we are attached to the earth and thus have to accept that whatever we decide there is a price to pay in relation to the earth itself. Spiritually we can find that our choices make it hard for us to decide at what point we have to make a stand, and in so doing the earth, and our attachment to it, will exact a price.

From time to time I have asked him whether it would be worth my while to pursue certain aspects of expertise. Sometimes he has said 'Yes,' sometimes 'No,' and sometimes, and more often, he says, 'It is a way of thought.' One of the questions I posed him was whether there was any reality to numerology, as it had interested me at one time, 'It is a way of thought' and I asked him how he would present the idea. As a result we have given classes under the heading of 'The Nine Laws of Spiritual Attunement'. This teaches that we have fully to understand these nine laws from every aspect, before we no longer need to reincarnate. The nine laws are –

1) Individuality

2) Quality

3) Self-expression

4) The will and balance
   – one, Nemerah says, of vital importance

5) Disciple into teacher

6) Love – This means in all its aspects and the beginning of understanding of real impersonal love

7) Inspiration

8) Renunciation and revelation

9) Selflessness.

Nemerah teaches at some length on all these laws. For each of us they expand in meaning through our own increased vision as we grow in spiritual understanding: so that we ourselves experience through various incarnations fully and comprehensively the self realisation that comes through knowledge. Always in the classes that we take or indeed when Nemerah himself is lecturing, there is an assessment of the personalities that are listening to him. So therefore there is never exactitude of repetition. For instance there is a series called 'The Uncharted Self', these are on-going classes usually of six to eight weeks based on the fact that we come to earth, having accepted the place that we are born, the parents that we have, and that many episodes that come within this life are foreordained. We have repeated the classes several times.

The format is guided visualisation. My part in it is difficult. I literally have to hold his power throughout the class which lasts for an hour and a half. I am always interested in the variety of his approach. The exercises he uses are governed by the collective ability of the whole class and vary from series to series. It always begins in the same way. The members are asked to visually create a chart. Then imagine themselves at the mouth of a river, in a craft of their own choosing. On their charts are various ports of call that are inescapable and others less defined. Looking at their charts, they also see that the river has smaller tributaries which lead into unknown territory. Using these tributaries and exploring the territory may enable them to find their way to a main port avoiding some of the unnecessary ones. Nemerah says the wonder of life is in the opportunities that come towards us at any given moment. If we use these opportunities constructively we can exceed our own spiritual expectations. We can escape certain confrontations because we can grow beyond the necessity of meeting them. These are the lesser points of call. For me this makes complete sense. For if everything was pre-ordained beyond any possibility of change, then what of the wondrous gift of free will?

The aspect of Nemerah's work that interests me most now is in his ability to relate to the inner need of the person sitting in front of me. To offer constructively, exercises both psychological, psychic and in some cases even physical, which combined with their concentrated will to help themselves will alleviate their condition of disturbance. The essential element is in the determination of the person concerned to succeed.

Another aspect of Nemerah's work comes under the heading which we call 'The Dark Angel'. In this we explore the negativity within the self that unconsciously holds on to the conditions that cause us problems. This is apparent at all levels, especially in our close personal relationships. We constantly repeat patterns of behaviour that engender stress in one another.

I see this sometimes when I am healing. Gently, if it is given me so to do, I may offer a suggestion as to why the illness is still there, only to hear the recipient re-avow the same thing in a different way.

I have listened to people who are obsessed psychically,

who say they wish to get rid of the condition. They will however make little effort to follow instruction as to how to close themselves to the invasion. It perhaps would seem less interesting to be without it.

We can find these negative areas within ourselves in many varying degrees. The Dark Angel within ourselves sometimes refuses to acknowledge and accept the cure, because the underlying factors would make life more difficult if we were seen to be whole.

The absolute interaction between the mind of ourselves and the greater source is an unfolding journey of exploration but it does mean that the one essential element is in the acknowledgement of self responsibility, there is nothing between ourselves and the God-source in totality. Therefore in acknowledging this we accept first of all the inner responsibility of ourselves and then, and only then, can we use the constructive powerful elements of spiritual interaction to which we all have access. Within the self lies the balancing structure of demand and acceptance but it is we who choose whether to accept what it has offered us and use it.

When used as a channel in this way I myself am conscious of compassion, of powerful impersonal projection of love. I realise that this is not mine, that I am the link that enables it to touch the measure of that moment. I also realise that there is within that area a three way purpose, that of Nemerah, myself and the recipient and that each of us holds within ourselves the divine ray, the right of inheritance because we are part of the God-source, and in however small a measure each of us wherever we walk carries that divine light within ourselves. I then accept with gratitude the privilege of being Nemerah's connecting link.

Through these years Nemerah has lectured on many subjects. He makes his views quite clear, almost always stating at the start of the lectures that these are his views according to his capacity to relate to his own unfoldment, and that those listening must accept or reject according to their inner note, that he says, is the truest note there is. 'If I say anything that does not ring true for you then reject it.'

It would be impossible to have had the association that I have had, and still have with Nemerah and to have remained untouched myself. What then have I learned through the years that we have been together? He has taken me from the acknowledgement of the Dark Angel within myself, through the understanding of the necessity of facing it.

I have accepted the psychological and mental aspects that created with my psychic ability the type of mediumship that I have. He has pointed the way to my conviction that life here has meaning, and death but a doorway to further experience.

Under his guidance there has been a gradual unfoldment within myself as I have assimilated his teaching. I know that life is a gift beyond price, for how we use it is its value in spiritual terms. I know that I respond as true for me, to the fact that we all have a place in the Divine plan, and that no other can usurp it. This gives to each of us the right to make of our life that which we will within the place we have accepted. Thus beyond that comes the awareness that the breathing essence of existence is part of an absolute whole. That we are one with God; thus we have access to Higher Intelligence or Cosmic Consciousness if we have the courage to search for it.

Step by step he showed me the danger and corresponding value of psychic energy, that the energy itself is a force. How we channel it creates the negative and positive poles. Used either way it is a collective and powerful force. Psychic laws follow a pattern, they only differ in degree. That point grasped, the horror of mob violence shows the depth of the negative, the wondrous selfless collective response in disasters, the positive. Therefore it would follow, given a nucleus of powerful psychic positive within a negative situation, violence could be lessened. That is at the extended level. More mundanely and beginning with myself, I have proved time and again, that if I have truthfully sent love towards a difficult situation it has lessened in impact.

I know that interchanging energies are co-existent and constant at innumerable levels. Just to be in the presence of certain people is enough to increase our own sense of peace and well-being. They carry an aura of enlightenment. The converse is also true. To live with someone who has an auric emanation that is depressive or destructive is a severe test of endurance. We can learn to combat part of the strain. There are many ways of doing this, dependent upon our own interactive energies, physical, mental and spiritual.

Some of the references Nemerah has made relating to energies I take on trust. I do not know. They ring true, I find them understandable and wholly believe they exist. He speaks of the true Indian mystic, who uses his life to regenerate the organic forces of the earth itself. Here is an extract from an answer he gave on being questioned on this subject.

> Through stillness and deep meditation the Yogi disciplines his body and his mind to co-exist in cosmic attunement. Through his understanding of the psychic laws he is able to exchange the meta-physical time element and create his own flow in time and space. His own philosophy creates within him his haven; so that his use of these laws to enhance the validity of his truth begins within himself. He is constant with the Divine flow of energy which unifies all Creation.
>
> The master in this field has attained awareness of being. He is part of universal love. He recognises wholeness, therefore, participating as he does in the life force which creates his own energy, he becomes a channel of light interchange. His life then, is part of a timeless echo; for in

this use of the life experiences that he is undergoing, he alternates in relating his physical body to the currents that hold him to the earth with the far greater knowledge of his enlarged mind that touches cosmic energy.

He takes himself into the contemplation of the deep seated energy reserves within the planet using them to purify and revitalise the earth surface itself. In the mountainous areas of the Himalayas, in certain areas of Peru, in the deserts such a master will exist, according to the spearhead of divinity that is his service. He is completely creative in that, because of his dedication, light energies that are conducted through him are as a power house of restoration and healing.

His knowledge of the greater laws embrace exactitude and acknowledgement of his place in time and gives momentum to his creativity.

He is governed by the reality of himself, as are we all. In terms of spiritual law, nothing can be that is unreal. He has mastery of himself in wholeness. Because of this, he also has mastery over his body and his emotions. He will need little sustenance of earthly food. He is not needful of personal love or of acknowledgement of personal contact. He holds love within his being.

To be in the presence of a soul who is a master in this way is to acknowledge an area of light that is wholly beneficial. It is projected and absorbed in the cycles of interchange within body, mind and spirit. This light absorption also holds a hereditary growth involvement for those of his disciples who follow him. He gives to them the acknowledgement of the laws that he commands. It does not necessarily at that time mean that they have reached a level of knowledge to use these laws, unless they themselves are in a state of equivalent grace. It may be many years of earth time before a disciple is able to release consciously the gift he holds in abeyance.

> Becoming conscious of the universe that is beyond ourselves is part of gradual growth. To search within ourselves for our own note of continuity is the level of attunement that can be used to express, within our present experience, purpose and fulfilment.

I have often been in the presence of people who project an aura of strength and spiritual enlargement which is recognisable and been blessed thereby. I have responded to a beautiful note of integrity while listening to others. I may not have agreed with the views they have expressed, or with their religious conviction, but I have been altered by their essence in some way.

Sometimes, busy with everyday tasks, I feel strength, warmth, vitality flooding my very being. I know then, that somewhere I am included in someone's loving prayers, or perhaps being sent Absent Healing. In some cases I am able to pin-point where it comes from. More often not; I just accept with profound gratitude the upliftment and joy that it brings. It is like 'a singing within the heart'.

Only once have I felt that I may have been in the presence of a master as described by Nemerah. It happened some while ago. I had not been asleep, but lying reviewing the events of the day. I began to feel pain at my feet which spread upwards through my body. I felt I was being forcibly pulled out of my body through my head. I heard Nemerah say 'Keep still and do not be afraid.'

I found myself standing in a small flattened plateau surrounded by high mountain peaks covered in snow. I judged it to be the Himalayas where of course it was day time. It was hot and the sun was brilliant. The ground was covered in grass, quite green. There were Indian people moving about, most of them wearing nothing but loin cloths. I did not notice any women. It was all so quick. The terrain nearby was very rocky, and seemed to provide some cavelike shelters. There was movement, an air of activity. I think food was being prepared by some.

Where I found myself standing there was complete stillness. I was about ten feet away slightly to the left of a man who was sitting crossed leg on the ground. He was young with long black hair, parted in the middle and shoulder length. His beard too was very black, and he was wearing a white garment with long wide sleeves. In front of him were five or six disciples sitting in the lotus position in absolute stillness. They were wearing orange cloths. From where I was I could not see his face fully. I knew that he could see me and was aware of me, and that no-one else was. There was a split second of recognition. I was effortlessly back in my body and fell almost instantly into a deep sleep. I cannot say when waking the next morning I was immediately aware of any change in myself. I have accepted since that I probably absorbed a necessary colour or vitality into my auric field. I have also accepted that masters are not of East or West. In reality they find us if it is part of the karmic pattern; we do not find them.

I have been shown gradually but consistently, that I alone am responsible for what I am or may become. Looking back I am saddened at my crass insensitivity to the needs of others. For the innumerable times I have wounded by word and deed. Above all of the growth opportunities I have wasted. I have also learned that to further waste time and energy in too much self recrimination is pointless. Guilt, like fear, is a valuable tool in the hands of the Dark Angel. Better by far repair the damage if I can, resolve that I will make every effort not to repeat the error, and let go consciously of the rest. For I know I cannot undo it. If I have incurred a spiritual debt I know at some time I will have a chance to repay that debt. I trust that I will pay it with love; willingly.

Balance in all things! Yes, we should examine ourselves and our motives from time to time. Yes we should, when we feel the necessity, take advantage of the innumerable therapies, teachings, groups, available to help us in our aim of self-examination. We should also remember that it is easy to cross the line into self-absorption.

I have found it difficult to come to terms with illness and suffering of individuals, and of the collective suffering and agony of parts of the world at large. Nemerah has led me through these areas very carefully and gently indeed. I feel now that I have the ability to comprehend a little. He advises: 'Do not dwell too much on the wide canvas. Look closely at the area which contains you. Do what you can to clean the picture there so that its colours shine clear.'

He always says if we dwell on the vast pattern of world misery, we become immersed in despair which is adding to the darkness of negation. Instead we should see the place in which our life is set and give all thought to that. We should, in our prayers or meditation, open our thoughts to asking of the source 'love towards the world and healing of its wounds'. For throughout the planet countless people of different beliefs and various ways will be doing the same thing. Then we should go about what is asked of us, in the best way we can, living each day as it comes, using our energies to give the best of what we are towards everything that we do. He stresses that we should enjoy happiness, laughter, kindness in full measure whenever we touch it. In so doing we increase our capacity 'as harbingers of light'; and in our turn release it in our interchange with others.

I have learned to value what my dreams tell me, to assess which strata of the mind released them. I have never worked with them deeply in the Jungian sense. Under Nemerah's tuition I know where they belong and when to take note of them. Sometimes the combination of factual with the dream visualisation is startlingly beautiful, the meaning unmistakeable.

One such concerned my mother-in-law. Our relationship

has not always been easy. When I was young I was often intimidated by her. She had a forceful personality, complete self assurance, natural dignity. Everything she undertook she did well. She was very very kind to a great many people. She accepted community responsibilities together with heavy home commitments. She looked after both her parents until they died; nursing them to the end. She was a keen gardener, a passionate animal lover. She sat on the council of several charitable committees and put the whole of her energy into helping achieve their aims. She played the piano to a very high standard of musicianship. Having sons, she knew a great deal about sport. She was a wonderful dressmaker, was always busy yet the home, of which she was the centre, did not have an air of fussiness.

It is true she had a live-in-maid whom she had taught to cook. A very good gardener, and various others who came in to help look after her mother who lived to be almost a hundred. Her father went up to his business in London by train every day until he was eighty-eight. Even with help she worked physically very hard herself. During the war she kept chickens and supplied eggs to friends rationed with her. She worked in the garden and did part of the cooking. She had incredible energy, self-discipline and self-control. She was, and still is, a stickler for time. Everything was done according to rule and a set pattern. If in trouble people automatically turned to her, they were never turned away. She could also at times be insensitive. She was domineering, autocratic to a degree, and could never admit she was mistaken about anything. She found it difficult to brook opposition of any kind. It took courage to face her temper and her tongue. However, once the incident was resolved it was over. She did not bear grudges. We couldn't have been more different. Inevitably there have been clashes over the years. On the other hand I have never asked her for help of any kind without receiving it in abundance. She has made curtains for me and covered chairs. I have turned to her time and again when worried over the children's illnesses and always been supported. She has been the most wonderful and loving grandmother. Financially she has been more than generous to us all. She made my children's party dresses, their fancy dresses for school plays, attended all their birthday parties, always arriving in time to help cut the sandwiches and do the work. When they were older she taught them dressmaking. Had them to stay for convalescent periods after illnesses. Took them to pantomimes, circuses, horse shows. They loved and still love her. She met their need at every age, all children and animals gravitated towards her. She is now ninety-nine and they still do!

When my husband died, it was a bitter blow. In retrospect I think I did not feel sufficiently for her. She had lost her other son during the war. Her husband, though separated for many years, remained a friend. He had died a few years previously and I know she had felt it keenly. She met the death of my husband with her usual fortitude and courage. I almost lost control in the car as we left the Crematorium. I felt my mother-in-law's hand firm as a rock on my arm: 'Stick it Elizabeth – stick it!'

She does not believe in any continuation of existence. Once or twice in the early days I tried to broach the subject. I was always met with a wall of resistance and she would change the subject. Recently I know she watched my television interview with Ean Begg; she has never referred to it. I have often found this sad.

When abroad I have the habit of bringing home small gifts, naturally including my mother-in-law. Then one day, in her practical way, she told me not to waste my money, she had more than enough of everything. Which was true, so I agreed and did not do so. Once after this, however, I was in Canada and choosing purses to bring home as presents. I was enjoying it. I had not seen any like them, and they were of all colours. My mother-in-law was not in my mind at all. Suddenly I heard my husband's voice, clearly, as though standing beside me. 'Take one home for my mother.' I did so. I would loved to have told her that she had a gift as I had had from her son, now living somewhere else. I knew I couldn't.

To return to my dream sequences. In the wall opposite my bed there is a long inset, about nine inches deep and ten feet long. At that time the walls were coloured a pale turquoise. I had a long low fitment running the length and the walls covered in hanging plants. When I awoke I literally looked on to flowers. In my dream I opened my eyes on the wall exactly as it was. I could see it dimensionally. The flowering geraniums became vibrant with life and intensity of colour. The wall behind misted, then disappeared. Beyond I was looking into a square room the side walls and ceiling covered in flowers of all kinds. That opened into another that I could see was equally beautiful. As I looked I knew I had earned that beauty in some way.

Then I was in my mother-in-law's home. Again exactly as it was. The same thing happened in quite different surroundings. First of all the wall, as it was, was edged in hanging baskets of flowers, then opened to reveal room after room of blossom as far as I could see.

I knew then, spiritually, she had earned far more than I, whatever she believed. I hope when my time comes I will have added to my rooms. As I think of the past, I have deep and lasting respect for her. She has never worn her heart on her sleeve. She has kept her sorrows to herself and worked through them. She has watched her kind of world deteriorating around her and accepted that with stoical courage. It is still impossible to make her do anything she doesn't want to do. She has instinctive wisdom. She recently said to me: 'I have sometimes been lonely. I have never been bored in the whole of my life.'

I believe that when asleep we do leave our bodies, and the experiences we have in that dream world of the astral are as factual as those we have here. The astral reality differs from the normal dream state, in that we are conscious of weight, smell, sound, touch, exactly as we relate to them here. For we are then functioning within the same frequency band. It is possible in the memory of the dream to distinguish and separate the altered states of consciousness.

I am often aware now of a continuation in the time sequence of such dreams. I know the people I am talking to, though we have never been together in my normal life. I have been within the same scene, I know the terrain. I am often with my husband. When with him in this way there is an interesting example of subconscious imagery projected into the occurrence. The last time I saw him on earth I kissed him goodbye through the lowered window of his car. Now as I am about to return to my body a car will appear. Either he will be in it and drive away, or I find both of us in a car and one or other will get out. Instantly the car appears I have a moment of regret. I know it is the end for the time being; almost instantly I wake.

To an extent, I am able sometimes to control events. A good exanple of this happened recently. A friend died leaving her husband shattered by grief. She had often been in my flat. In my dream I heard the door bell ring. I realised instantaneously that I was functioning in the astral. The dream had solidity and dimension. I opened the door, and there was my friend. She had died in her sixties. She looked twenty years younger. 'I can't stay long, someone will be coming to take me back.' Together we turned into my bedroom. We began to look at my clothes and knick-knacks, chattering and laughing as we did so, inconsequently passing comments just as we might have done in the past. She seemed to be listening for something. The door bell pealed again 'That will be for me,' she said. We went to open the door. I could feel her behind me. Just before I opened the door I felt her leave me. I moved quickly back to the bedroom. She was standing by the window with a sense of urgency. 'She wants me to wake up' I thought. I forced myself consciously back into my body. It was an effort but I was wide awake when I heard her call her husband's name. I was able to write and tell him: 'I was awake when I heard her call your name. I was not asleep!'

The most salutary lesson I have had to learn is to accept how very little I really know. As I come to terms with just one facet of understanding I think how crassly stupid I have been not to have grasped and understood it sooner. I would have behaved so differently. The answer is, of course, that the keys to unfoldment can only come when we ourselves are ready to unlock the corresponding door. We cannot be more than we are at any given time. I see so many young people who have come to terms with psychic and spiritual awareness, so much earlier in their lives than I ever did. I find this heartening. In retracing my steps in this way I realise that many of the names, so important to me, are now history in this field. They continue their lives elsewhere. Their work is well documented and accounts can be found in all the relevant libraries. The College of Psychic Studies houses one of the best. The new names bring their ongoing energies. Uri Geller, Matthew Manning come immediately to mind, as being in the public eye.

In the small arena of the College itself I am fascinated by the continuing threads. Working there still is my own teacher, Ivy Northage. Within the confines of the College we both teach. Certain things I learnt from her I will never forget. I still pass them on to my own students in almost the same words. I have benefited immeasurably from her tuition and the wisdom of Chan. As I have explained earlier our pathways have diverged as I have accepted wholly my guidance from Nemarah. His methods differ from those of

Chan, so that the two streams have run side by side. In the intervening years both Ivy's students and mine have become my colleagues, working professionally in their own right. Before my time at the College is completed I hope to have others standing beside them. They do not, and will not, repeat my pattern; but obey their own directive and extend their horizons. In some cases I watch with interest the changes that have already taken place. The energies are reaching into seas uncharted by me. I find this rewarding and inspiring. Who knows how far they may go? Or what wonders they may find? As Nemerah says, the miracles of today are unlikely to be the miracles of tomorrow.

There is much talk of the destruction of the planet. If we look upon the devastation we have caused upon the earth, it indeed seems possible. In attunement with Nemerah it is certainly not inevitable. He has stated frequently that if such destruction was fore-ordained emissaries such as himself, would not be allowed to waste their energy.

In having learnt a little about the co-ordination of light energy within the mediumistic quality, the way ahead, to my mind, holds infinite possibilities. For instance, the corresponding expression of materialisation could be a form of picture projection above the medium's head. Scientifically we can produce the hologram. Then mediumistically if we could increase our mental projection to reach the high frequencies that would be needed, could we not reach a stage, perhaps, of scientific and discarnate mind co-operation? Water divining is an accepted fact. It is comparatively easy to envisage such a gift being increased to a far greater potential, so that water could be made available in countries where they are desperate for it. Imagine a highly charged positive mediumistic quality allied to a human heart of true compassion, reaching a unification with a soul of magnitude, and that power used to heal, to regenerate skin tissue perhaps. Think of the implications in relation to burn victims undergoing painful skin grafting operations. Think of the possibility of the rejuvenation of brain cells of those with Alzheimer's disease. The imagery is endless. The line between fantasy and vision is another of very fine balance. But before a dream becomes reality there has to be vision. A visionary projects possibility; whether its echo returns as reality remains to be seen.

I truly believe that all these things are possible. I also know that I must retain a balance with everyday living. That is the only way I, personally, can grow. I have been a wife and daughter. I am a mother, a grandmother, a sister, a friend, an acquaintance, a passer-by. All these relationships carry responsibilities, some more obvious than others. If I listen to Nemerah independently I'm forced to the conclusion that the most important aspect of my life lies in the gift of myself towards its living. As I have tried to show, my mediumship is dependent upon the kind of psychic combination I have as an instrument. The only thing that I can give is the way in which I serve it. This also applies to all the other facets of my life. Mediumship is part of my life, it is not the whole of it. There are many points of growth potential. I am given the right of selection as to how I balance them and how I express, within the whole of the picture, the different variants.

Once, long ago, I was caught in a traffic jam in the country. As far as my eye could see were green fields covered in marguerites and buttercups, wave upon wave of them. In my mind's eye I can see it vividly now. I can also recall the thought that crossed my mind. The wonder of all that beauty had been untouched by human hand. They were wild flowerings, their seeds carried by the wind, nurtured in the soil, blessed by the sun, had grown in the ceaseless harmony of life itself. We, the casual passers-by, had been caught for a moment within that harmony, we had been given a vision of beauty with eyes that could see the immensity of loveliness that is ours at any given moment in time. We had been presented with a moving picture of continuation, an understanding of the true relationship of all life, God's breath within eternity. Inexorably the traffic moved, my moment of vision was taken from me. The memory and understanding remains.

Seen in the light of spiritual illumination our lives become a wondrous journey of unfolding exploration, with many strata of expression. If we believe in reincarnation then we know we have chosen our manner of entry into this life. We have accepted our parentage which will bring its own inheritance of gender, colour, creed and kind. From the first moment of our consciousness we will be contained within this structure until we can assume greater responsibility for our own growth in thought and ideology. We will, nevertheless, be held by ties of blood and the bonding of love, or otherwise, that contains us. We will have within the immediate structure of the family situation an opportunity to increase the bonding of love, in the relationship of parent, child and sibling, or perhaps to release a bonding that had contained servitude, cruelty and oppression.

If we think of a lifetime of interaction with growing circles of relationships of all kinds the permutations are endless, each permutation carrying within it the seeds of our thoughts, words and deeds. Extend beyond that, not to one lifetime, but to many lifetimes, the inner harmonic of our own note of attunement, exerting its sound ray through timelessness in space, to find a re-echo through all the graduations of the final orchestration which takes us back, eventually, to the source of life itself. Think then of a body housing a soul of enlightenment, one who has reached an understanding of temporal and spiritual law, his horizons so vast that countless numbers are affected by his decisions and his deeds. To accept such a life takes immense courage, for the responsibilities are hazardous in the extreme, for surely he will be contained in the shock waves of collective karma, affecting the universe and beyond that to cosmic consciousness.

Such thoughts are difficult for the finite mind to sustain consistently, for we reach a point where there are no words to express what we have understood. Better by far to keep our feet on the ground and give full value to the unfolding journey of our present life. Each life is a priceless gift in its entirety, another doorway leading to growth potential, governed by the interchange of love between people. It magnifies and reflects the spark of divinity that lies, however deeply hidden, within the human heart; that miraculous spark which has survived the repeated senseless onslaught of man's inhumanity to man throughout eons of time. That wondrous spark that can ignite momentarily into flame, lighting our way into spiritual expansion. Let us then accept the gift unconditionally, use it with wisdom, and account it full measure in all our journeyings through sunshine and shade. We are its keeper, with the freedom to hide or share our treasure. Only we can diminish or increase its value. Ours is the choice.

May I end in the way Nemerah often brings to a close his discourse?

Remember we are of light, we are of love, we are of God. May God be with you my friends.